TIME
FOR KIDS

GRAMMAR RULES!

By Ann Weil

Illustrated by John Joven

PRODUCED BY

DOWNTOWN BOOKWORKS INC.

PRESIDENT: Julie Merberg
EDITORIAL DIRECTOR: Sarah Parvis
EDITORIAL ASSISTANT: Sarah DiSalvo
AUTHOR: Ann Weil
ILLUSTRATOR: John Joven
DESIGNED BY: Georgia Rucker Design

PUBLISHER: Bob Der
MANAGING EDITOR, TIME FOR KIDS MAGAZINE: Nellie Gonzalez Cutler
EDITOR, TIME LEARNING VENTURES: Barbara E. Collier

PUBLISHER: Jim Childs
VICE PRESIDENT, BRAND & DIGITAL STRATEGY: Steven Sandonato
EXECUTIVE DIRECTOR, MARKETING SERVICES: Carol Pittard
EXECUTIVE DIRECTOR, RETAIL & SPECIAL SALES: Tom Mifsud
EXECUTIVE PUBLISHING DIRECTOR: Joy Butts
DIRECTOR, BOOKAZINE DEVELOPMENT & MARKETING: Laura Adam
FINANCE DIRECTOR: Glenn Buonocore
ASSOCIATE PUBLISHING DIRECTOR: Megan Pearlman
ASSISTANT GENERAL COUNSEL: Helen Wan
ASSISTANT DIRECTOR, SPECIAL SALES: Ilene Schreider
SENIOR BOOK PRODUCTION MANAGER: Susan Chodakiewicz
DESIGN & PREPRESS MANAGER: Anne-Michelle Gallero
BRAND MANAGER: Jonathan White
ASSOCIATE PREPRESS MANAGER: Alex Voznesenskiy
ASSOCIATE PRODUCTION MANAGER: Kimberly Marshall
ASSISTANT BRAND MANAGER: Stephanie Braga
EDITORIAL DIRECTOR: Stephen Koepp

SPECIAL THANKS: Katherine Barnet, Jeremy Biloon, Rose Cirrincione, Jacqueline Fitzgerald, Christine Font, Jenna Goldberg, Hillary Hirsch, David Kahn, Amy Mangus, Amy Migliaccio, Nina Mistry, Jonathan Rosenbloom, Dave Rozzelle, Ricardo Santiago, Adriana Tierno, Vanessa Wu

For information on TIME For Kids magazine for the classroom or home, go to TIMEFORKIDS.COM, or call 1-800-777-8600. For subscriptions to SI Kids, go to SIKIDS.COM, or call 1-800-889-6007.

Published by TIME For Kids Books, an imprint of Time Home Entertainment Inc. 135 West 50th Street New York, NY 10020

1 QGT 13

ISBN 10: 1-60320-954-9
ISBN 13: 978-1-60320-954-0

TIME For Kids is a trademark of Time Inc.

We welcome your comments and suggestions about TIME For Kids Books. Please write to us at: TIME For Kids Books, Attention: Book Editors, P.O. Box 11016, Des Moines, IA 50336-1016. If you would like to order any of our hardcover Collector's Edition books, please call us at 1-800-327-6388 (Monday through Friday, 7 a.m. to 8 p.m., or Saturday, 7 a.m. to 6 p.m., Central Time).

CONTENTS

PARTS OF SPEECH

Words play different roles in a sentence. And parts of speech—like nouns, pronouns, verbs, and conjunctions—tell us what those roles are. When you understand parts of speech, you understand how words fit together to make sense in a sentence.

NOUNS

Common and Proper Nouns

Nouns are words that name people, places, and things. A noun can also name an idea or a feeling, like joy, anger, and confusion. Spotting the nouns in a sentence helps you know what the sentence is all about. Let's look at two kinds of nouns: **common nouns** and **proper nouns**.

A **common noun** names any person, place, or thing.

boy	computer	city
girl	fish	house
day	fork	subway

A **proper noun** names a specific person, place, or thing. Days of the week, months, and holidays are also proper nouns. Proper nouns begin with a capital letter. Some proper nouns contain more than one word. Each important word begins with a capital letter.

Elmo	Statue of Liberty	Vilas Middle School
Uncle John	Monday	Groundhog Day
Antarctica	October	World War II

Look at these sentences about the same class trip. Notice that using proper nouns can make the writing more specific and interesting.

Common Nouns	Proper Nouns
My **teacher** took the class to the **museum** to see a **painting**.	**Ms. Jenkins** took the class to the **Museum of Modern Art** to see *The Starry Night* by **Vincent Van Gogh**.

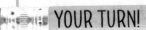

YOUR TURN! — *Show What You Know*

Circle the common nouns and underline the proper nouns in the sentences below.

- Nick helped Mr. Preston make a sign for the carnival in Springdale.

- Linda knows that education is important in South Africa.

- There is no school on Monday because it is Presidents' Day.

- Grandpa Jack was too young to fight in the Vietnam War.

- Kim and Anna are identical twins.

- Jack did his report on penguins in Antarctica.

YOUR TURN!

LOOK OUT!

Not all dog-breed names are capitalized. The names that come from proper nouns, such as specific geographical locations, begin with capital letters.

- Yorkshire terrier
- English bulldog
- Labrador retriever
- Newfoundland
- Saint Bernard
- Great Dane

BUT

- boxer
- pug
- beagle
- poodle
- dachshund

A Proper Matchup

Each common noun in the left column goes with a proper noun in the right column. Draw a line to show each match.

Common Nouns	Proper Nouns
boy	Taj Mahal
road	November
dog	Mount Everest
president	Fourth of July
holiday	Fred
continent	Oakdale Lane
month	Chihuahua
monument	North America
mountain	Barack Obama

Know Your Nouns

Caitlyn spilled orange juice on her keyboard, and now the shift key won't work.

Circle the proper nouns in Caitlyn's message below. Then write them on the lines below with the correct capitalization. Remember, some proper nouns contain more than one word.

I went to camp wamsutta with my brother eric.
We were gone for the whole month of july.
My counselor's name was felicity, which I found out means happiness! I wrote postcards to my parents and grandpa jim every saturday during rest period after lunch. I told them I want to come back to this camp next year.

1. _____   4. _____

2. _____   5. _____

3. _____   6. _____

NOUNS

Singular and Plural Nouns

Now let's look at nouns in another way. Is there only one or more than one?

A **singular noun** names *one* person, place, or thing.

A **plural noun** names *more than one* person, place, or thing.

From Noun to Nouns

How do you make a noun plural? Changing a singular noun to a plural noun can be as easy as adding an *-s* at the end. This simple rule applies to many common nouns. Fill in the blanks.

card ▶ *cards*

kite ▶ *kites*

banana ▶ *bananas*

valley ▶ _____

reef ▶ _____

nose ▶ _____

toe ▶ _____

toy ▶ _____

Add *-es* to form the plural of singular nouns that end in *s, ss, sh, ch, x,* and *z.*

gas ▶ *gases*

dress ▶ *dresses*

dish ▶ *dishes*

lunch ▶ _____

watch ▶ _____

beach ▶ _____

fox ▶ _____

buzz ▶ _____

To form the plural of nouns ending in a consonant and *y,* change *y* to *i* and add *-es.*

baby ▶ *babies*

city ▶ *cities*

candy ▶ *candies*

library ▶ _____

country ▶ _____

family ▶ _____

berry ▶ _____

penny ▶ _____

LOOK OUT!

Some people have last names that end with a *y.* Don't change the spelling of their name. Just add a final *-s* to show the noun is plural.

- Mr. and Mrs. Kaminsky live next door.
- The Kaminskys are good neighbors. correct
- The Kaminskies are good neighbors. incorrect

Irregular Plurals

Some nouns have special plural forms.

one man ▸ two *men*

one foot ▸ many *feet*

one person ▸ lots of *people*

one child ▸ several _____

one mouse ▸ three blind _____

one tooth ▸ all my _____

Sometimes when a singular noun ends in *f* or *fe,* the letter *f* is changed to a *v* before the *-es* is added to form the plural.

knife ▸ *knives*

wife ▸ *wives*

leaf ▸ *leaves*

calf ▸ _____

hoof ▸ _____

wolf ▸ _____

One Deer; Two Deer; Oh, Dear

Some nouns have the same singular and plural form. This is most common in the names for animals. Here are a few examples.

deer ▸ deer

moose ▸ moose

sheep ▸ sheep

fish ▸ fish

salmon ▸ salmon

trout ▸ trout

YOUR TURN!

How Many?

Write the singular of these irregular plural nouns.

Irregular Plural	Singular
tomatoes	_____
oxen	_____
thieves	_____
geese	_____
feet	_____
loaves	_____

NOUNS

Possessive Nouns

A **possessive noun** shows that a noun has or owns something.

To form the possessive of a *singular* noun, add an **apostrophe** (') and *-s.*

> **This phone belongs to Austin.**

> **Austin's phone is broken.**

This rule holds true even if the name ends with the letter *-s.*

> **Carlos left his notebook in the cafeteria.**

> **Mr. Smith returned Carlos's notebook.**

To form the possessive of a *plural* noun that ends in *-s,* add an **apostrophe** (') to the end of the word.

> **Three doctors share an office.**

> **The doctors' office is next to the hospital.**

To form the possessive of a *plural* noun that does *not* end in *-s,* add an **apostrophe** (') and *-s.*

> **My grandparents like to put on plays for children.**

> **They started a children's theater.**

Make It Possessive

Fill in the blanks with the possessive form of the underlined nouns.

- <u>Mary</u> is wearing a hat. _____ hat has a feather in it.

- It took a long time for the <u>jury</u> to reach a decision. The _____ verdict was guilty.

- Kendall has twin <u>sisters</u>. His _____ birthday is May 15.

- The <u>architect</u> drew up plans for a new house. There were three balconies in the _____ plans.

- The animal shelter had four cages for <u>rabbits</u>. The _____ cages were in the back room.

- Three <u>women</u> went out for lunch together. A waiter brought the _____ menus.

- The <u>dog</u> jumped over the fence. The _____ collar came off.

LOOK OUT!

These sentences look a lot alike, but they have different meanings. Getting your grammar right can help you make it clear how many people and how many objects you are referring to.

My aunt's bike is red.

My aunts' bike is red.

My aunts' bikes are red.

The Last Word on Last Names

Add **-es** to last names that end in **-s** to make them plural.

Then add a final **apostrophe** (') to make the plural possessive.

- Mr. and Mrs. Jones have a dog.

- The Joneses love to walk their dog.

- The Joneses' dog loves to chase cats.

PRONOUNS

Subject Pronouns

Pronouns are words that stand in for nouns.

I	you	she	we
me	he	her	they
us	him	it	them

Look at these sentences.

Logan can skate like a pro.

He can skate like a pro.

The second sentence has the same meaning as the first. *He* stands in for the proper noun *Logan*.

Logan is the subject of the sentence, so the pronoun that stands in for Logan must be a subject pronoun.

A **subject pronoun** takes the place of a subject noun.

Subject Nouns	Subject Pronouns
Patty likes to shop.	**She** likes to shop.
Jill, Ellen, and I ate cupcakes.	**We** ate cupcakes.
The **boys** bought a game.	**They** bought a game.
The **dog** stole my homework.	**It** stole my homework.

Like nouns, pronouns can be singular or plural. A singular subject pronoun stands in for a singular subject noun, and a plural subject pronoun stands in for a plural subject noun.

The birds flock to the new bird feeder.

They flock to the new bird feeder.

Subject Pronouns	
Singular	**Plural**
I	we
you	you
he/she/it	they

The Right Pronoun for the Job

Be careful to use the right pronoun when a sentence has a **compound subject**.

Amelia and I walked home together.

compound subject

She and I walked home. *correct*

Her and I walked home. *incorrect*

If you're not sure which pronoun to use, try the sentence without *and I*.

Her walked home doesn't sound right at all!

When the pronoun *I* is used with another noun in the subject, *I* always comes last.

Ben and I were finalists in the spelling bee. *correct*

I and Ben were finalists in the spelling bee. *incorrect*

Say it out loud. I and Ben. Doesn't that sound awful?

More Pronouns

Most pronouns, like *he, she,* and *it,* stand in for a specific person or thing. You know who or what the pronoun stands in for in the sentence. These pronouns are different. They are open ended. Someone could be . . . anyone.

someone	anyone	everyone	something
somebody	anybody	everybody	no one

Everyone is here today.

Anyone could have made this mess.

Someone cleaned the kitchen.

LOOK OUT!
These pronouns are all singular, even *everyone* and *everybody*. It's important to remember this so you use the right verb form.

15

PRONOUNS

Object Pronouns

If the noun you want to replace with a pronoun
is the object in a sentence, use an **object pronoun**.

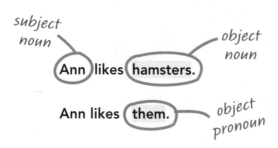

Because *hamsters* is plural, you use
a plural object pronoun.

Object Pronouns	
Singular	**Plural**
me	us
you	you
him/her/it	them

Here are some examples of object pronouns taking the
place of object nouns.

Object Nouns	Object Pronouns
Ben broke a cup. Ben blamed Kevin.	Ben broke it. Ben blamed him.
Hannah builds robots. The robots obey Hannah.	Hannah builds them. The robots obey her.

The sentences above show an object pronoun that comes after an action verb.
Object pronouns also come after words that show a relationship, such as *for, with,*
and *about.* (Words that show a relationship are called **prepositions,** and you can check
them out on page 48.)

Dad baked a birthday cake for my brother. ▶ Dad baked a birthday cake for him.

I went to the soccer game with Gwyneth. ▶ I went to the soccer game with her.

Pablo wrote his report about astronauts. ▶ Pablo wrote his report about them.

Pronouns with Compound Objects

Be careful to use the correct pronoun when a sentence has a **compound object**.

Caroline thanked (Jack and me.) *correct*

Caroline thanked Jack and I. *incorrect*

compound object

My parents drove him and us. *correct*

My parents drove he and us. *incorrect*

If you're not sure which pronoun to use when you have a compound object, try the sentence with only one pronoun at a time. Does *Caroline thanked I* sound right to you? How about *My parents drove he?* When you say them out loud, they just sound wrong.

Pick Your Pronouns

YOUR TURN!

- Louisa and _____ are going shopping.
  (me/I)

- Kyle and _____ are at the arcade.
  (them/they)

- _____ went out to dinner together.
  (Us and them/We and they)

- Dad told _____ to clean my room.
  (me/I)

- _____ and Jackson were science partners.
  (Her/She)

- Mom already picked _____ up.
  (them/they)

- My grandparents took _____ to a movie.
  (us/we)

PRONOUNS

This popcorn is mine. All mine!

Possessive Pronouns

A **possessive pronoun** can take the place of a **possessive noun.** Like a possessive noun, a possessive pronoun shows who or what owns (or possesses) something.

my	our
mine	ours
its	your
her	yours
hers	their
his	theirs

Some possessive pronouns always come before a noun.

My dog is sleeping.

Your dog is chasing a squirrel.

Her dog is wearing a pink sweater.

Other possessive pronouns always stand alone.

Hers won the blue ribbon.

Mine came in second.

Yours came in third.

LOOK OUT!

Possessive nouns have an apostrophe:

• Jeanette's book is on the table.

But possessive pronouns do not:

• This book is hers.

Reflexive Pronouns

Use a **reflexive pronoun** when the subject and object of a sentence are the same.

I don't trust **myself** around chocolate-chip cookies.

Dad helped **himself** to a second piece of pie.

See how reflexive pronouns "reflect" back on the subject.

Reflexive pronouns end in *-self* or *-selves*.

myself	ourselves
yourself	yourselves
himself	themselves
herself	
itself	

LOOK OUT!

Some people get a little confused about reflexive pronouns and use made-up words. Don't fall into the fake word trap.

himself correct

themselves correct

ourselves correct

hisself incorrect

theirself incorrect

theirselves incorrect

ourself incorrect

YOUR TURN!

Reflect on This

Complete each sentence with the correct reflexive pronoun.

- Susan bought _____ a birthday present.

- I taught _____ how to play the piano.

- No one will win if they all vote for _____.

- We helped _____ to dessert.

- After his haircut, Jake did not recognize _____ in the mirror.

LOOK OUT!

Never substitute reflexive pronouns for subject or object pronouns.

- My parents and 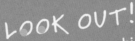 went camping together. correct — subject pronoun
- My parents and myself went camping together. incorrect
- The hall was decorated by Fiona and me. correct — object pronoun
- The hall was decorated by Fiona and myself. incorrect

VERBS

Types of Verbs

Verbs tell us what someone or something is or does.

An **action verb** tells what someone or something *does*. *Jump, run,* and *write* are action verbs. *Think* and *sleep* are action verbs, too, even though they don't sound so active.

> The teacher draws a circle on the chalkboard.
> Hannah raked the lawn.
> Jimmy is jumping rope on the sidewalk.

A **linking verb** tells what someone or something *is*. It *links* the subject of a sentence to some information about it. It can describe something's state of being. The most common linking verbs are forms of the verb "to be" (*is, am, are*). *Seem, look,* and *feel* are linking verbs, too.

> The rabbit is gray with white patches.
> Jerome looks tired.
> Alison feels hungry.

LOOK OUT!

Some verbs can be used as either action verbs or as linking verbs.

ACTION VERBS:
- Kiara smelled the roses.
- The chef tasted the beef stew.
- Bill looked all over the house for his glasses.

LINKING VERBS:
- The roses smelled sweet.
- The beef stew tasted great.
- The pizza deliveryman looked angry.

Verbs Are Very Important!

Every sentence must have a verb. Some action verbs can be one-word sentences.

Help!

Wait!

Jump!

Spotting Action Verbs

Read the paragraph below. Find and circle all 16 action verbs.

Charlotte and Darren danced in their school's talent show. First, Charlotte twirled around the room. Then Darren leaped across the stage. He hopped and jumped all around. Charlotte and Darren swayed to the music and sang along with the lyrics. When the music stopped, they stopped. The other students stood while they clapped and cheered. Charlotte and Darren smiled at each other. They reached for each other's hand, and then they bowed and left the stage.

VERBS

Writing with Verbs

When you write, think carefully about the verbs you choose. Some verbs can provide more information and give the reader a clearer picture of what is happening. For example, a person who is stomping is making noise, and a person who is tiptoeing is not. A person who is pigging out is eating a great deal, and a person who is nibbling is not.

Use **VIVID** Verbs!

Verbs tell the action in a sentence. When you write, make sure to choose vivid verbs that help your reader picture exactly what is happening. Compare the two short paragraphs below. Notice how *raced, shrieked* and *disappeared* are more vivid than *went, said*, and *left*.

1   After school, Alfie and Jim went to get the school bus. But before they could get aboard, some other children began throwing snowballs at them. "Watch out," said Alfie. Alfie and Jim put down their backpacks and picked up handfuls of snow. Within minutes, the children were all covered in white, and the bus had left.

2   After school, Alfie and Jim raced to catch the school bus. But before they could jump aboard, some other children began hurling snowballs at them. "Watch out," shrieked Alfie. Alfie and Jim threw down their backpacks and scooped up handfuls of snow. Within minutes, all the children were coated in white, and the bus had disappeared.

10 Vivid Verbs to Use Instead of ...

Walk	Look	Eat	Say
hike	admire	chomp	declare
meander	gaze	devour	express
march	glare	gobble	murmur
run	glance	inhale	read
skip	glimpse	munch	reply
shuffle	inspect	nibble	scream
stomp	ogle	pig out	shriek
strut	peek	scarf	state
tiptoe	stare	snack	whisper
wander	spy	swallow	yell

Verb Swap

Replace the words in red type with more vivid verbs. If you are stumped, choose from the words in the hint box on the right.

I looked out the plane window. Just then, a bolt of lightning came near the plane. I held the arm of the seat and closed my eyes. The plane landed on the runway. What a ride that was!

YOUR TURN!

What Are Your Favorite Verbs?

Think of all the actions you perform in a day, such as going to gymnastics, playing video games, or making a craft project. What descriptive verbs can you use to describe what you like to do? Write them below.

_____

_____

_____

_____

_____

_____

_____

VERBS

Action Shots

Look at these photos. If you were to tell a story based on each photo, what cool action verbs would you use? Write the verbs near their photo.

YOUR TURN!

_____   _____

_____   _____

_____

_____

_____

_____

VERBS

Present, Past, and Future Tenses

The **tense** of a verb tells the time when something happens.

A verb in the **present tense** says something is happening now.

> Claire is happy.
> My brother rides the school bus.
> We take all our cans and bottles to the recycling center.

A verb in the **past tense** says something has already happened. You can simply add **-ed** to many verbs to show past tense.

> I walked to the store and back to buy milk.
> Molly learned how to ride horses last summer.
> Roselle played the lead role in last year's school play.

A verb in the **future tense** says something is going to happen. To write about the future, use the helping verb **will.** (For more on helping verbs, go to pages 30–31.)

> We will sell sunflowers at the farmers' market next Saturday.
> Jon and Eric will shovel the snow when the blizzard is over.
> A new store at the mall will open next month.

Shall We?

The word *shall* was once commonly used instead of *will*, especially with the pronouns *I* and *we*. Now, most people use only *will* with future-tense verbs. *Shall* is still used occasionally when asking questions.

- **Shall we go to the zoo?**
- **What shall we have for dinner?**

In the Past? Or in the Future?

> **Fill in the blanks in this chart.**

REGULAR VERBS

Present Tense	Past Tense (add -ed)	Future Tense (add will)
walk	walked	will walk
call		
appear		
stay		
climb		
cook		

Changing Tenses

Some verbs require more spelling changes than simply adding **-ed** and **will** when the tense changes from present to past or future. Here are a few rules to keep in mind when changing a present-tense verb to past tense.

If a verb ends with **-e,** drop the **e** and add **-ed.**

I like banana splits. ⤵ I liked banana splits when I was younger.

The cooks bake a different kind of cake every week. ⤵ Last week, they baked a chocolate cake with vanilla frosting.

If a verb ends with a consonant and a **y**, change the **y** to **i** and add **-ed.**

Babies cry. ⤵ Molly cried when she was a baby.

We try new foods at dinner. ⤵ Last night, I tried a hot pepper.

LOOK OUT!

These rules apply to many verbs, but there are exceptions to the rules. The past tense of the verb to fly isn't flied. It's flew! These verbs are called irregular verbs. We'll look at the irregular verb to be on the next page.

Sometimes you need to double the final consonant before adding **-ed**.

I shop with my mom. ⤵ Last month, we shopped for new school clothes.

My grandparents hug me every time I visit. ⤵ Yesterday, Grandma hugged me for a whole 10 seconds.

Consistency Is Key

When you are writing, make sure you use the same tense for actions that happen at the same time.

past tense *past tense*

Garrett (opened) the door and (picked up) the newspaper. correct

present tense *present tense*

Garrett (opens) the door and (picks up) the newspaper. correct

past tense *present tense*

Garrett (opened) the door and (picks up) the newspaper. incorrect

VERBS

Irregular Verbs

Irregular verbs break all the rules. They have special forms for singular and plural subjects. They also have special forms for the present tense and the past tense.

You already know a lot of irregular verbs. When you write or say *I am*, you are using the irregular verb "to be."

	Singular	Plural
PRESENT tense of the verb *to be*	I am a doctor. You are a teacher. She is happy.	We are busy. You are very tall. They are from Ohio.
PAST tense of the verb *to be*	I was at school. You were hungry. He was silly.	We were tired. You were on the bus. They were on time.

YOUR TURN!

To Be or Not to Be . . .

Read the sentences below. Underline the forms of the verb *to be*.

Gina and her family are in Boston on their vacation. They are interested in the history of the old city. It is more than 350 years old. In those early days, some streets of Boston were only dirt paths. There were no traffic lights on any corners! "That was my favorite trip ever," Gina said when they got home.

Now fill in the correct form of the verb *to be* in each blank.

I _____ surprised to see that Boston _____ a modern city. There _____
  (past)   (present)   (present)
tall buildings made of steel and glass right next to smaller, older brick buildings.

Yesterday, we _____ so tired of walking that we took the subway to see
                       (past)
Paul Revere's house. Boston's subway _____ the oldest subway system in
                                 (present)
the United States! Our guide at Paul Revere's house _____ from Ohio,
                                             (past)
just like us! There _____ people here from all over the world!
         (present)

More Irregular Verbs

Like the verb *to be*, there are other irregular verbs that have special forms for the past tense.

He rings the bell.

» **He rang the bell yesterday.**

They catch fireflies.

» **Last night, they caught lots of fireflies.**

I write in my diary every night.

» **I wrote an essay last week.**

Show and Tell

> **Read the sentences below.**
> **Write the correct form of the verb.**

Last week, Ms. Goldman _____ to the
(speak)
class about being kind to animals. The last time she

spoke to us, she _____ a dog with her.
(bring)
This time she _____ up an iguana in a cage
(hold)
to show the class! Some people were frightened,

but Ms. Goldman _____ there was
(say)
nothing to worry about. She _____ us
(tell)
that iguanas get along well

with people. She even

_____ an iguana as a
(keep)
pet when she was a little girl.

Some IRREGULAR Verbs

PRESENT TENSE	PAST TENSE
begin	began
bite	bit
bleed	bled
blow	blew
break	broke
bring	brought
build	built
catch	caught
choose	chose
come	came
creep	crept
dig	dug
do	did
draw	drew
drive	drove
eat	ate
fall	fell
feed	fed
fight	fought
freeze	froze
get	got
give	gave
hold	held
make	made
ring	rang
run	ran
say	said
tell	told
write	wrote

VERBS

Main Verbs and Helping Verbs

Some verbs are made up of more than one word. A verb can be made up of a **main verb** and a **helping verb.** The main verb shows action, and the helping verb works with the main verb. Forms of the verb *to be* are often used as helping verbs.

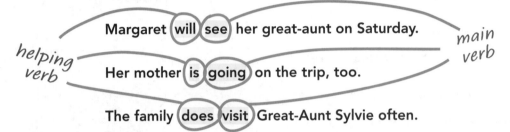

helping verb

Margaret (will) (see) her great-aunt on Saturday.

Her mother (is) (going) on the trip, too.

main verb

The family (does) (visit) Great-Aunt Sylvie often.

Some Common Helping Verbs

have	does	is	should	will
has	could	are	been	would
had	am	was	were	shall

YOUR TURN!

Family Photos

Read the sentences below. Draw one line under the helping verbs. Draw two lines under the main verbs.

Great-Aunt Sylvie has lived in the same house all her life. On Saturday, Margaret and her mother will visit there. They are taking recent family photos with them, and Great-Aunt Sylvie will show them an old family album. Margaret is looking forward to the visit.

Past Tense with Helping Verbs

One way to show something that has already happened is to use a helping verb with the **past tense** of the main verb.

helping verb — I (have) (talked) to him on the phone three times already. — main verb

Tanya (has) (practiced) piano every day this week.

YOUR TURN!

Quick Learner

Read the sentences below. Circle the helping verbs. Underline the main verbs.

Jennifer has enjoyed listening to music for a long time. She has studied piano for one year. I have heard better players, but they have all studied for many years. Jennifer has become a very good player in only a year. She has always wanted to play as well as famous piano players. She has promised to learn my favorite song. Jennifer and her friends have talked about playing for an audience. They have mentioned this plan to many people!

Forming a Band

Read the sentences below. Fill in the correct form of the helping verb in each blank.

For months now, Dave and Michael _____ wanted to start a band. Dave _____ played the drums for several years. Michael received a guitar on his birthday and _____ plucked its strings every day since then. The boys _____ started regular practice sessions together. They are still looking for a singer, and I _____ thought about trying out for the position! I _____ wanted to sing in a band for a long time!

31

ADJECTIVES

Types of Adjectives

Adjectives describe people, places, and things. They tell more about nouns and pronouns. Some adjectives tell what kind or how many. Others describe color, shape, or size. Vivid adjectives help bring writing to life by telling what something looks like, sounds like, smells like, tastes like, or feels like.

Adjectives often come before a noun or pronoun.

Alice has purple (pants.) — *noun*

Adjectives may follow a linking verb.

The subway (is) noisy. — *linking verb*

Some **number adjectives** tell exactly how many.

She had three pencils.

Indefinite adjectives do not give an exact number.

Isabelle saw several movies over the summer.

Proper adjectives are formed from **proper nouns, such as the names of countries or continents and languages.** Like proper nouns, proper adjectives begin with a capital letter.

Grandma took me to a French restaurant.

Religious words are also proper adjectives.

Judith found a picture of a Buddhist temple.

Here are a few other examples.

- Amish
- Catholic
- Christian
- Hindu
- Jewish
- Lutheran
- Muslim
- Protestant

Proper Noun	Proper Adjective
France	French
England	English
Spain	Spanish
China	Chinese
America	American
Italy	Italian
Japan	Japanese
Asia	Asian

Adjectives and Articles

Adjectives may be placed after the word *a, an,* or *the.* These short words are called **articles.**

The dog has a wet nose. *article*

Articles are used before nouns or before words that describe a noun. Use *a* and *an* when the noun is singular. You can use the article *the* for either singular or plural nouns. Use *a* when the word begins with a consonant sound. Use *an* when the word begins with a vowel or a silent **h.**

the mouse (singular)

the mice (plural)

a crown (before a consonant)

a house (before the letter *h* with a consonant sound)

an apple (before a vowel)

an hour (before a silent *h*)

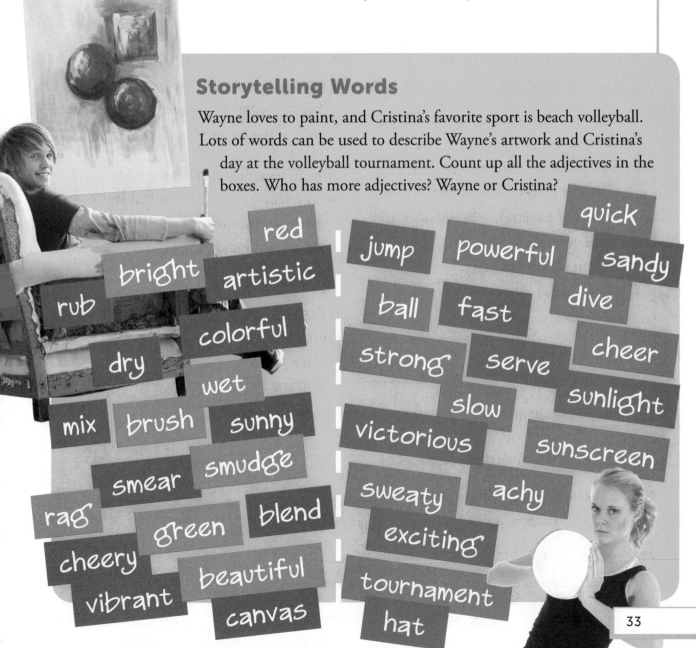

Storytelling Words

Wayne loves to paint, and Cristina's favorite sport is beach volleyball. Lots of words can be used to describe Wayne's artwork and Cristina's day at the volleyball tournament. Count up all the adjectives in the boxes. Who has more adjectives? Wayne or Cristina?

rub bright red artistic

colorful

dry wet

mix brush sunny

smear smudge

rag green blend

cheery beautiful

vibrant canvas

jump powerful quick sandy

ball fast dive

strong serve cheer

slow sunlight

victorious sunscreen

sweaty achy

exciting

tournament hat

33

ADJECTIVES

Comparing with Adjectives

Comparative adjectives compare nouns. Many comparative adjectives end in **-er.**

> My father is taller than my mother.
>
> A plane goes faster than a car.
>
> My cousin is stronger than I am.

Superlative adjectives compare more than two nouns. Many superlative adjectives end in **-est.**

> I am the tallest student in my class.
>
> A rocket is the fastest way to go.
>
> My cousin is the strongest kid at our school.

Creating Comparatives and Superlatives

You can add the suffixes **-er** and **-est** to many adjectives to create comparative and superlative forms.

> low ‣ lower ‣ lowest
>
> quick ‣ quicker ‣ quickest
>
> bright ‣ brighter ‣ brightest
>
> hard ‣ harder ‣ hardest
>
> rich ‣ richer ‣ richest
>
> old ‣ older ‣ oldest

Sometimes you need to double the final consonant before adding **-er** and **-est.**

> hot ‣ hotter ‣ hottest
>
> big ‣ bigger ‣ biggest
>
> thin ‣ thinner ‣ thinnest

Sometimes you need to change a final **-y** to an **i** before adding the correct suffix.

> crazy ‣ crazier ‣ craziest
>
> funny ‣ funnier ‣ funniest
>
> silly ‣ sillier ‣ silliest

If the adjective already ends in **-e,** don't add a second **e.**

> cute ‣ cuter ‣ cutest
>
> close ‣ closer ‣ closest
>
> fine ‣ finer ‣ finest

Describe and Compare

Fill in the blanks with a comparative or superlative adjective. Superlative adjectives compare three or more things.

My backpack is heavy, but her backpack is _____.

All kittens are small, but the runt of the litter is the _____.

My room is clean, but my sister's room is _____.

The neighbors have three smelly dogs, and the one named King is the _____.

When Do You Need "More"?

Use *more* and *most* with a three-syllable (and longer) adjective instead of adding a comparative or superlative suffix.

beautiful ➡ more beautiful ➡ most beautiful

intelligent ➡ more intelligent ➡ most intelligent

important ➡ more important ➡ most important

Many two-syllable adjectives also use *more* and *most* instead of a comparative or superlative suffix.

careful ➡ more careful ➡ most careful

pleasant ➡ more pleasant ➡ most pleasant

active ➡ more active ➡ most active

LOOK OUT!

Some two-syllable adjectives can use either *more* and *most* or suffixes in their comparative and superlative forms.

clever
cleverer ➡ cleverest
more clever ➡ most clever

gentle
gentler ➡ gentlest
more gentle ➡ most gentle

friendly
friendlier ➡ friendliest
more friendly ➡ most friendly

quiet
quieter ➡ quietest
more quiet ➡ most quiet

YOUR TURN!

Make the Most of It

Complete the chart below.

Adjective (Positive Form)	Comparative Form	Superlative Form
tall	taller	tallest
crazy	crazier	craziest
beautiful	more beautiful	most beautiful
dirty		
interesting		
safe		
peaceful		
awesome		
proud		
enormous		
smooth		

ADJECTIVES

Irregular Adjectives

There are no rules for irregular adjectives. You just need to learn them, as you do irregular verbs. You probably use some of these adjectives every day.

good, well (healthy) ▶ better ▶ best

bad ▶ worse ▶ worst

many ▶ more ▶ most

far ▶ farther ▶ farthest

For more on when to use *good* and when to use *well*, see page 126.

LOOK OUT!
These are NOT words. Really!

- badder   • baddest
- funner   • funnest

From Bad to Good . . .

Don't confuse the adjectives "worse" and "worst." **Worse** is the comparative form of *bad*. **Worst** is the superlative.

My cold is worse today than it was yesterday, but it is not the worst cold I have ever had.

The comparative form of *good* is **better.** The superlative form of *good* is **best.**

This game was better than the last one, but it is not the best game I have ever played.

A Person Cannot Be Dead-er

Some adjectives are absolute. If two lines are parallel, they never meet. Two lines cannot be *more* parallel or *less* parallel than another pair of parallel lines. They are either parallel or they are not. Likewise, something is dead or it is not. To say something is *more dead* doesn't really make sense (except maybe in zombie movies).

Here are some other "absolute" adjectives.

unique   single   perfect

Comparative Crossword Challenge

Is this a good crossword puzzle? Perhaps it is better than the average crossword puzzle. Maybe it is the best crossword puzzle you've ever done. Fill in the answers to the crossword clues below to weigh in. Remember, some adjectives use suffixes (-er, -est). Some use *more* and *most*. Make sure to use the answer that fits inside the puzzle.

ACROSS
3. The comparative form of good
5. The comparative form of tiny
8. The superlative form of quick
9. The comparative form of big
10. The comparative form of dirty
12. The superlative form of cute
15. The superlative form of beautiful
18. The superlative form of strong
19. The comparative form of fine
21. The comparative form of young
22. The superlative form of clever

DOWN
1. The superlative form of silly
2. The superlative form of brave
4. The comparative form of easy
6. The comparative form of icy
7. The superlative form of cold
8. The superlative form of quiet
9. The superlative form of bright
11. The comparative form of gentle
13. The comparative form of simple
14. The comparative form of active
16. The comparative form of long
17. The superlative form of shiny
20. The superlative form of bad

ADJECTIVES

Adjectives and Commas

You can use more than one **adjective** to describe a noun or pronoun. Sometimes you need commas between multiple adjectives, and sometimes you don't.

Use a comma when the adjectives could be joined by "and" without affecting their meaning.

> **It was a long, boring documentary.**
> *(The documentary was long and boring.)*

> **Susan is an honest, true friend.**
> *(Susan is honest and true.)*

You should also be able to reverse the order of the adjectives.

> **It was a boring, long documentary.** *(Zzzzzzz!)*

> **Susan is a true, honest friend.** *(That sounds good, too!)*

Do not use a comma when one or more of the adjectives forms a unit with the noun.

> **Mom's purple wool sweater is ugly.**
> *(A purple and wool sweater does not sound right.)*

> **My little baby brother is so cute!**
> *(Little and baby brother does not sound right either.)*

You wouldn't reverse the order of the adjectives in the phrases "wool purple sweater" and "baby little brother," so you do not need a comma between them.

YOUR TURN!

Comma Commander

> Do any of these sentences need a comma between the adjectives? Put a ✓ next to the sentences that are fine without commas. Underline the sentences that need commas between the adjectives.

- Sheila bought a cute red miniskirt at the mall yesterday.

- Ms. Pearson has a busy demanding job as a veterinarian.

- That restaurant serves the lightest fluffiest pancakes I ever tasted.

- We just drove past an old stone house.

- After sledding, Tyson took a long hot shower.

- Jane and I just had a stupid pointless argument over nothing.

Order of Adjectives

Sometimes the order of adjectives isn't important. Other times it is. Think about the difference between "three empty water bottles" and "empty three water bottles." But knowing which adjective to put first isn't always so obvious. It often helps to say a phrase out loud to see if it sounds right. "Little old lady" sounds more natural than "old little lady."

This chart shows the usual order for some types of adjectives.

How Many	Opinion	Size	Age	Shape	Color
one	silly	big	new	long	red
two	horrible	small	old	round	purple
several	interesting	little	young	square	blue

Proper Adjectives	Material	Purpose
French	cotton	sleeping
English	paper	walking
Buddhist	wooden	writing

There were two silly big old round purple Swiss wooden walking sticks at the yard sale. I found one horrible small old square red cotton sleeping bag in the giveaway box. While I was there, someone actually bought several interesting little antique rectangular wooden writing desks.

Uh. Okay.

YOUR TURN!

Which Comes First?

Rewrite the sentences using the adjectives to describe the underlined noun. Be sure to write them in the correct order and use commas when necessary.

Last summer, we went on a trip. (camping, exhausting, long)

_____

I want a cake. (three-layer, chocolate, birthday, huge)

_____

She wore shoes. (size-8, leather, Italian, black)

_____

ADJECTIVES

Be Descriptive

What adjectives would you use to describe the people and objects in these photos?

YOUR TURN!

_____   _____

_____   _____

_____

_____

_____

_____

_____ _____

_____ _____

_____

_____

_____

_____

ADVERBS

Types of Adverbs

An **adverb** tells how, when, or where something happens. Adverbs may come before or after the verb (or verb phrase) they modify (have an effect on). Many adverbs end in *-ly.*

Some adverbs tell *how* an action takes place.

> **She quickly ate her lunch.**
>
> **James carefully opened the glass cabinet.**
>
> **Priscilla plays the harp beautifully.**

Some adverbs tell *when* or *how often* an action takes place.

> **They are leaving for the airport soon.**
>
> **School is closed today because of the snow.**
>
> **My grandparents often visit.**

Some adverbs tell *where* an action takes place.

> **Dmitri hoped his friends would be there.**
>
> **During recess, the children played outdoors.**
>
> **A bird flew through the open window.**

It's easy to get adjectives and adverbs confused. Both describe something else. One way to tell them apart is to compare adjectives with adverbs that mean the same thing and end in *-ly.*

Jack is (brave.) *adjective*

Jack climbed the beanstalk and (bravely) fought the giant. *adverb*

Adjective	Adverb
angry	angrily
brave	bravely
cheerful	cheerfully
happy	happily
merry	merrily
polite	politely
quick	quickly
slow	slowly

Other Adverbs

Here are some adverbs that do not end in *-ly.*

- ahead
- always
- below
- everywhere
- here
- later
- nearby
- never
- not
- sometimes
- there
- today
- tomorrow
- upstairs
- very
- well

Adverbs Everywhere

Adverbs usually modify a verb, but they can also modify an adjective or another adverb.

adverb Isabelle ran (very) (quickly) to catch the school bus. *adverb*

adverb Lucas looked (almost) (everywhere) for his homework. *adverb*

adverb She is (really) (ready) to go this time. *adjective*

YOUR TURN!

Try It in a Sentence

Change these adjectives to adverbs that end in *-ly*. You may need to make some spelling changes (like *happy* to *happily*) to write each adverb correctly. Then use each adverb in a sentence of your own.

even | evenly |

She divided the cookies evenly among all the children.

graceful | |

_____

mysterious | |

_____

nervous | |

_____

lazy | |

_____

awkward | |

_____

eager | |

_____

ADVERBS

Adjectives vs. Adverbs

You already know lots of adjectives and adverbs. Show off some of your descriptive powers in these fun activities.

DESCRIPTIVE DUOS

Draw a line to match up adjectives with the nouns that they could describe.

gems	gentle
pool	sparkly
salsa	flaky
soldier	slimy
snake	boiling
snail	fierce
pastry	greasy
mother	spicy
cactus	old-fashioned
tiger	hissing
water	spooky
mirror	brave
jack-o'-lantern	victorious
pizza	prickly
team	shallow

Adverb Jumble

Some adverbs fell into a blender and got all mixed up. Unscramble each mixed-up adverb. This brainteaser is a tough one, so we've provided a hint for each word.

daylitemime = __ __ __ __ __ __ __ __ __ __ __

Clue: "I said, right now!"

yuledeepnxct = __ __ __ __ __ __ __ __ __ __ __ __

Clue: "That's a surprise!"

rullygear = __ __ __ __ __ __ __ __ __

Clue: Right on schedule

nailfly = __ __ __ __ __ __ __

Clue: At last!

yooshfill = __ __ __ __ __ __ __ __ __

Clue: Silly me!

futtyorlean = __ __ __ __ __ __ __ __ __ __ __

Clue: You are so lucky!

tallcandyice = __ __ __ __ __ __ __ __ __ __ __

Clue: I didn't mean to do that!

saylaw = __ __ __ __ __ __

Clue: Every single time!

soyajulle = __ __ __ __ __ __ __ __ __

Clue: Green with envy

hulyring = __ __ __ __ __ __ __ __

Clue: I ate the whole thing!

lganiry = __ __ __ __ __ __ __

Clue: I'm so mad at you!

recently
slowly
honestly
rapidly
clumsily
secretly
jealously
happily

45

CONJUNCTIONS

JOINING IDEAS

Coordinating conjunctions join ideas that are independent. Each phrase can stand alone as a complete sentence.

Erin ran faster than Greg. She won the race.

Mom bought all the ingredients. We had everything we needed to bake a cake.

Coordinating Conjunctions

A **conjunction** is a word that connects words, phrases, or entire sentences. Conjunctions are sometimes called "joining words" because of the role they play in a sentence. The three most common conjunctions are *and*, *or*, and *but*. They are **coordinating conjunctions**.

Use the conjunction *and* to add information or combine related ideas.

> Jack **and** Jill went up the hill.

> I like to go swimming **and** rock climbing.

Use the conjunction *or* to show a choice.

> I want a bunny **or** a ferret.

> You can go swimming **or** rock climbing.

Use the conjunction *but* to show a difference.

> I like broccoli, **but** my sister doesn't.

> Paul already knows how to swim, **but** Louis is still learning.

The conjunction *so* shows that the first idea caused the second idea.

> Erin ran faster than Greg, **so** she won the race.

> Mom bought all the ingredients, **so** we had everything we needed to bake a cake.

YOUR TURN!

Bringing Sentences Together

> Which of these coordinating conjunctions is the best choice for joining each of the sentence pairs below?

and   or
but   so

- I like fruit, _____ I like cookies.

- Jeb studied for the math test, _____ he aced it.

- Katie packed her bag, _____ she was ready to go.

- Nathan speaks Spanish and English, _____ Luis speaks only Spanish.

- The school bus was late, _____ Alice was late for school.

- Lisa slept over at Grandma's house, _____ her brother stayed home.

- Peggy Sue likes scary movies, _____ Billy does not like them.

Subordinating Conjunctions

Subordinating conjunctions show other relationships between phrases in a sentence.

The conjunctions *before* and *after* tell when.

> She took a shower **before** she went swimming.
>
> She went rock climbing **after** she went swimming.

The conjunctions *because* and *since* tell why.

> I did not go swimming **because** it was raining.
>
> **Since** Aaliyah missed the bus, Mom drove her to school.

The conjunctions *if* and *unless* tell under what condition.

> I will go swimming **if** it is not raining.
>
> **Unless** it is a snow day, Tuesday will be a regular school day.

Common Subordinating Conjunctions

There are many more subordinating conjunctions than there are coordinating conjunctions. Here are a few of the most commonly used subordinating conjunctions.

after	just as
although	once
as	rather than
as if	since
as long as	so that
as much as	than
as soon as	that
as though	though
because	till
before	unless
even	until
even if	when
even though	whenever
if	where
if only	whereas
if when	wherever
if then	whether
in order that	while

YOUR TURN!

Use Conjunctions When You Write

Write a paragraph about yourself using as many conjunctions as you can. Circle the coordinating conjunctions, and underline the subordinating conjunctions.

_____

_____

_____

_____

_____

_____

_____

PREPOSITIONS

Common Prepositions

about	beneath	out
above	beside	outside
across	between	over
after	down	past
against	during	through
along	for	to
around	from	toward
at	in	under
before	inside	until
behind	of	up
below	on	with

Using Prepositions

A **preposition** shows a relationship between words in a sentence. A preposition can make a big difference in the meaning of a sentence.

I'll meet you **before** school.

➤ I'll meet you **after** school.

The mouse is **on** the desk.

➤ The mouse is **under** the desk.

LOOK OUT!

The word *but* can function as both a preposition and a conjunction (but not at the same time!).

• Everyone *but* you already saw that movie. (preposition)

• You like comedies *but* not thrillers. (conjunction)

How can you tell? If you can replace the word *but* with *except*, it is being used as a preposition.

Pick Out the Prepositions

Read the sentences below, and see if you can spot all 10 prepositions. Remember that there may be more than one preposition in a single sentence.

Our school has a chess club. It meets on Tuesdays after school for an hour. The members study the rules of the game and talk about different strategies for playing well. Before a tournament, the club members meet for practice games. During the games, the players concentrate hard. I am thinking about joining the chess club.

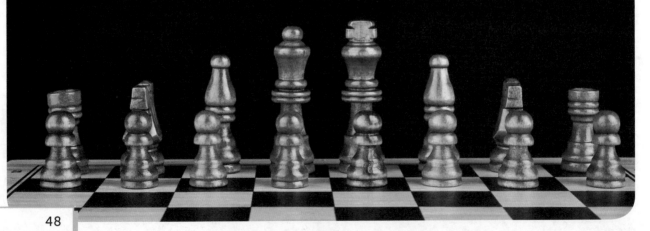

Field Trip Fill-In

Read the sentences below, and fill in each blank with a preposition. Keep in mind that sometimes there is more than one correct choice.

This morning, all the Nature Club members climbed _____ a bus bound _____ our town's nature preserve. Once there, everyone hiked the marked trails _____ the woods. Mr. Cindiric was _____ the group. He is an expert _____ all the different birds, animals, and plants _____ this area. He taught us to look _____ our heads for birds' nests. We saw a mother bird feeding her babies, but _____ the tree, we saw some tiny broken eggs. As the group walked _____ the shore of the lake, Mr. Cindiric showed us a raccoon's paw prints.

From Start to Finish

Follow the prepositions to find a path from start to finish.

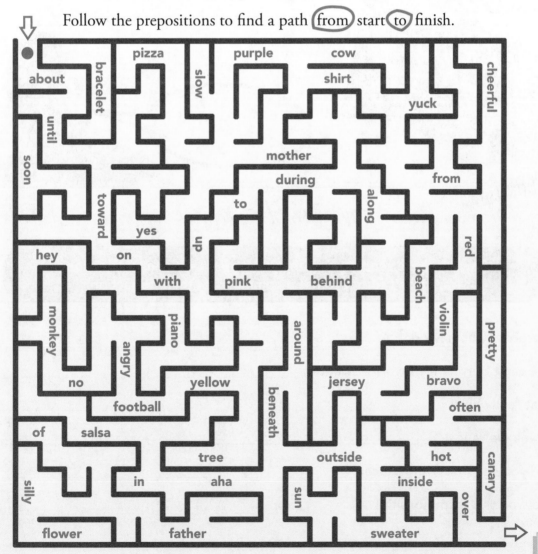

INTERJECTIONS

Inserting Interjections

An **interjection** is a word or phrase that is a command or shows emotion. An interjection can stand alone as a sentence with end punctuation.

> **Wow!**
> **No way!**
> **Oh, my!**

Interjections may come at the beginning of a sentence.

> **No,** I do not like mustard on my eggs.
> **Careful,** that pan is very hot.
> **Thanks,** I was about to drop it on my foot.

Interjections add emotion, but they do not change the meaning of a sentence. You could rewrite each of the sentences above without the interjection, and the meaning of the sentence would remain the same.

Common Interjections

Aha	Oops
Bravo	Ouch
Brrrrrr	Shhh
Gee whiz	Ugh
Hey	Uh-oh
Hooray	Um
My goodness	Well
Oh, come on	Whoops
Oh, no	Yuck

LOOK OUT!
Interjections are usually used only in conversations and informal writing.

Shhh!

YOUR TURN!

Oh, No! I Forgot My Interjection!

Rewrite these sentences so that each starts with an interjection. Wait! Don't forget to use a comma after the interjection.

I forgot my homework. _____

You can't borrow my favorite sweater. _____

That really hurt! _____

I think we're lost. _____

Did you see that flying saucer? _____

We won the championship! _____

A Word with Many Functions

Sometimes a word can function as an interjection in one sentence and another part of speech in a different sentence.

That was a (great) meal.

Here, great is an adjective.

(Great,) I would love to take a break.

Here, great is an interjection.

Great!

You can tell that the word *great* is an interjection in the second sentence because it has no grammatical relationship with any of the other words in the sentence. You could take it out of that sentence without changing the meaning.

YOUR TURN!

Movable Interjections

The interjection in each of these sentences can function as a different part of speech. Write a second sentence that shows how.

Well, that was interesting.

Jack didn't feel well after eating five hot dogs with everything on top.

Good, I was hoping you would come with me.

_____

My, you have grown!

_____

Help, there's a spider in the sink!

_____

No, you may not ride on the roof of the car.

_____

CRAFTING AN EXPERT SENTENCE

Sentences are the building blocks of language. We express our ideas through sentences when we speak and write.

SENTENCES

What Makes a Sentence

- A sentence is a group of words.
- A sentence expresses a complete thought.
- A sentence begins with a capital letter.

Types of Sentences	Examples
A **statement** tells something. It ends with a period.	**Animals come in different sizes.**
A **question** asks something. It ends with a question mark.	**Can you name the largest animals in the world?**
A **command** (imperative sentence) tells someone to do something. It usually ends with a period.	**Be careful around wild animals.**
An **exclamation** shows strong feeling. It ends with an exclamation point.	**That whale is huge!**

Sentence Spotter

As you read the sentences below, decide what kind of sentence each one is. Write an *S* above each statement, a *Q* above each question, a *C* above any command, and an *E* above an exclamation.

Can you name an animal that is bigger than an elephant? I will give you a hint. It can swim. Now do you know what it is? It is the blue whale. Did you know a blue whale can grow to be 100 feet long? It can weigh as much as a dozen elephants. That's a lot! When it is born, a baby blue whale can be as large as an elephant. Don't try to play with one!

Identifying the Subject and the Predicate of a Sentence

The **subject** of a sentence is the person, place, or thing the sentence tells about.

The **predicate** tells what the subject is or does.

Even the shortest, simplest sentences have a subject and a predicate.

subject — (Kangaroos)(jump.) — predicate

Most sentences are longer than two words. It is useful to know how to find the subject and predicate in these longer sentences.

The **complete subject** includes all the words in the subject.

The **complete predicate** includes all words in the predicate.

complete subject — (Red kangaroos)(are the largest kind of kangaroo.) — complete predicate

MIX AND MATCH ZEBRA TALES

Match each complete subject on the left with a complete predicate on the right. Draw a line between them to make a complete sentence. Be sure that the sentences make sense.

Herds of zebras	confuse predators.
A zebra's blended stripes	can reach 40 miles per hour.
The running speed of a zebra	was hunted to extinction by humans.
A zebra's powerful kick	are dangerous predators of zebras.
Human hunters	is forceful enough to kill a lion.
One species of zebra	were mostly brown and had few stripes.
These extinct zebras	have ways of defending themselves against predators.

SENTENCES

Subjects and Predicates

The **simple subject** is the main word in the complete subject. It is almost always a noun or pronoun. The **simple predicate** is the verb.

simple subject   All (kangaroos) (are) marsupials.   simple predicate

A **compound subject** has two or more simple subjects with the same predicate.

compound subject   (Kangaroos and koalas) are marsupials.

A **compound predicate** has two or more simple predicates with the same subject.

Koalas (eat and sleep) in trees.   compound predicate

YOUR TURN!

Play I Spy with Simple Subjects and Predicates

In each sentence below, (circle) the simple subject, and <u>underline</u> the simple predicate.

Harry Houdini became a great escape artist. He picked many different kinds of locks. People tied him in ropes and handcuffs. Houdini always escaped. His most dangerous trick happened underwater. People locked him in chains. They then threw him into a river. Houdini escaped from the chains. Then he swam to the surface of the water. Many people watched this trick.

Complete Subjects vs. Compound Subjects

<u>Underline</u> the complete subject in each sentence. (Circle) the compound subjects.

Warm-blooded animals are able to keep their body temperature constant. Birds and mammals are warm-blooded. These animals can turn the food they eat into energy. This complicated process creates heat. Some warm-blooded animals sweat when they get too hot. Dogs and wolves pant to cool down.

YOUR TURN!

Complete Predicates vs. Compound Predicates

Underline the complete predicate in each sentence. Circle the compound predicates.

Cold-blooded animals have the same temperature as their surroundings. They move and hunt in hot weather. Chemicals in their bodies react quickly to help their muscles move. These reactions slow down as the outside temperature drops. So they move slowly or stay still at low temperatures.

LABELING LESSON

Read these sentences about plants, animals, and other living things.

Write CS next to the sentences that have a compound subject.

Write CP next to the sentences that have a compound predicate.

Write B next to the sentences that have BOTH a compound subject and a compound predicate.

Do not write anything next to the sentences that have neither a compound subject nor a compound predicate.

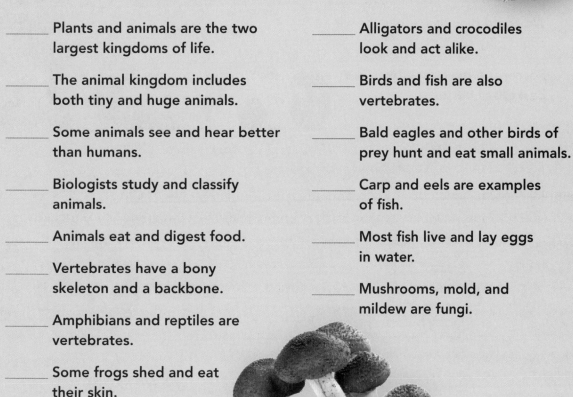

_____ Plants and animals are the two largest kingdoms of life.

_____ The animal kingdom includes both tiny and huge animals.

_____ Some animals see and hear better than humans.

_____ Biologists study and classify animals.

_____ Animals eat and digest food.

_____ Vertebrates have a bony skeleton and a backbone.

_____ Amphibians and reptiles are vertebrates.

_____ Some frogs shed and eat their skin.

_____ Alligators and crocodiles look and act alike.

_____ Birds and fish are also vertebrates.

_____ Bald eagles and other birds of prey hunt and eat small animals.

_____ Carp and eels are examples of fish.

_____ Most fish live and lay eggs in water.

_____ Mushrooms, mold, and mildew are fungi.

SENTENCES

Types of Sentences

A **simple sentence** with one subject and one predicate contains one complete thought.

> I like basketball.

I like basketball is also an **independent clause**. It is complete and can stand alone.

A **compound sentence** is two simple sentences with two subjects and two predicates joined together. A compound sentence contains two complete thoughts. It has two **independent clauses**. You can join two simple sentences into a compound sentence with a comma followed by *and*, *or*, or *but*.

> I like basketball. Luis likes soccer.
>
> I like basketball, and Luis likes soccer.
>
> We could play basketball, or we could play soccer.
>
> Soccer is a fun game, but I like basketball better.

A **complex sentence** has two related ideas joined by a conjunction other than *and, but,* or *or.*

> I eat a snack as soon as I get home.
>
> I eat a snack because I am hungry.
>
> I eat a snack before I do my homework.

In the sentences above, *as soon as*, *because*, and *before* are examples of subordinating conjunctions. For more on subordinating conjunctions, see page 47.

Which Parts Are Dependent?

Complex sentences include an independent clause and a **dependent clause.**
A dependent clause, such as "as soon as I get home," cannot stand alone as a sentence.

Independent clauses — I eat a snack / as soon as I get home. — **Dependent clauses**

We are shopping / because I need a new sweater.

She jogs / before she does her homework.

A dependent clause can come before or after the independent clause. If the dependent clause comes first, use a comma.

Until you clean your room, / you're grounded. ← *Use a comma.*

You're grounded / until you clean your room. ← *Do not use a comma.*

Prepositional Phrases

A **prepositional phrase** is a preposition, its object, and any words that describe the object. (For more on prepositions, see page 48.)

People like to run along the river.   *preposition*

All of those runners enjoy the scenery.   *preposition*

A prepositional phrase can be placed at the beginning, middle, or end of a sentence. A sentence may contain more than one prepositional phrase.

Of all the runners, Emma ran up the hill the fastest.

The shoes of the runners are specially designed by a famous company.

YOUR TURN!

Can It Stand Alone?

Underline the dependent clauses in the sentences below.
Circle the subordinating conjunctions.

I stayed home from school because I had a cold. After I took my medicine, I felt better. I napped while Mom did chores. Even though I was still a little sick, Mom took me with her to the supermarket. I pushed the shopping cart while Mom chose the vegetables. Mom bought three bags of oranges because they were on sale. She would have bought oranges even if they were not on sale. Oranges are good to eat when you have a cold.

Pinpointing Prepositional Phrases

Read the sentences below. <u>Underline</u> the prepositional phrases. Keep in mind that a single sentence may have more than one prepositional phrase.

In the spring, a famous race is run in the city of Boston. The name of the race is the Boston Marathon. Runners come from many countries. The hardest part is running up the hills. The athletes run through several towns on their way to the city. Along the route, the athletes run with different people. Supporters on the street cheer for the dedicated competitors.

SENTENCES

Fragments

A **sentence fragment** is a group of words that are written as a sentence but are missing a subject or predicate (or both). A fragment is **not** a sentence.

The yellow and black school bus. ← *fragment*

This is a fragment because it is missing a verb.

Leaving before the test was over. ← *fragment*

This fragment is missing a subject. It might be altered to become a full sentence in many ways. Here are two options.

She left before the test was over.

She made a scene and stormed out of class today, leaving before the test was over.

LOOK OUT!

Some sentences can be complete with just a subject and a verb.

Joe cooks.

But often, a sentence that includes only a subject and a verb does not express a complete idea. For example, *Joe takes* makes sense as a sentence sometimes. But in most cases, the reader is left wondering what exactly Joe took.

USE YOUR MENTAL CHECKLIST

Whenever you write a sentence, check to see if it is complete. Ask yourself, "Who or what is doing something?" If the sentence answers that question, then it has a subject. Next, ask yourself, "What is the subject doing?" If you can answer both questions about your sentence, then you have written a complete sentence.

YOUR TURN! — Put On the Finishing Touches

Make complete sentences from the fragments below by adding either a subject or a predicate (or both). Then (circle) the complete subject, and underline the complete predicate.

Lots of people.

(Lots of people) like pop music.

Is new and improved.

Three scoops of vanilla ice cream.

My brother's feet.

Is purple with white polka dots.

Run-On Sentences

A **run-on sentence** has two or more sentences that should be written separately.

Patsy found her slipper the dog had chewed on it. ← *run-on sentence*

You can correct a run-on sentence by separating two complete ideas into two sentences.

Patsy found her slipper. The dog had chewed on it. ← *two sentences*

You can also correct a run-on sentence by rewriting it as a compound or complex sentence using a conjunction.

complex sentence

Patsy found her slipper, (although) the dog had chewed on it.

conjunction

YOUR TURN!

Best Buddies

Underline the run-on sentences in the paragraph below. Then rewrite the paragraph correctly on the lines below. Keep in mind that there may be more than one way to correct each run-on sentence.

Ethan and Luke grew up together they went to the same school. The boys liked the same sports they played soccer in the fall and basketball in the winter. Some people thought the boys were brothers they looked so much alike. Ethan's mother and Luke's mother were best friends. The two families even went on vacations together sometimes they went camping.

_____

_____

_____

_____

_____

_____

AGREEMENT

Subject-Verb Agreement

We've already seen that the subject of a sentence (usually a noun or pronoun) can be singular or plural (see pages 10–11). Most verbs have different forms for singular and plural subjects. If the subject is singular, use the singular form of the verb. If the subject is plural, use the plural form.

These present-tense verb forms agree with most singular and plural nouns.

The simple past tense of many verbs is the same for both singular and plural subjects. For example:

I baked cookies.

We baked cookies.

He baked cookies.

They baked cookies.

Singular	Plural
takes	take
drives	drive
cries	cry
was	were
is	are
has	have
does	do

Staying the Same

Here are some past-tense verbs that are the same for singular and plural subjects. Can you think of some more?

cried	forgot	spoke
drove	held	stuck
_____	_____	_____
_____	_____	_____

We baked cookies.

I baked cookies.

Use Your Instincts

Most native English speakers do not need to remind themselves: "Make sure the subject and verb in this sentence agree!" They already do it automatically when they speak.

singular subject — My (cat)(likes) mice. *correct* — singular verb

singular subject — My (cat)(like) mice. *incorrect* — plural verb

plural subject — (Cats)(like) mice. *correct* — plural verb

plural subject — (Cats)(likes) mice. *incorrect* — singular verb

plural subject — (They)(are) playful. *correct* — plural verb

plural subject — (They)(is) playful. *incorrect* — singular verb

YOUR TURN!

Make It Work!

(Circle) the subject, and underline the verb in each sentence. Next to each subject and verb, write **S** for singular or **P** for plural. If the subject and verb in a sentence agree, mark that sentence with a ✓ at the end. If the subject and verb do not agree, mark an **X**, and write in the correct verb form.

Jill walk to school with her mother.

_____

They gets to school at 8:30.

_____

Jill's big brothers rides the bus to the high school.

_____

Science is the first class of the day.

_____

Jill sits next to Jen in science class.

_____

Both girls likes science class.

_____

Jen take better notes than Jill.

_____

Sometimes Jill copy Jen's notes after class.

_____

Horace talks during science class.

_____

Mr. Harrison remind Horace to be quiet.

_____

AGREEMENT

Compound Subjects

When a compound subject is joined by the word *and*, use a plural verb.

compound subject — The (cat and the dog) (sleep) on the front porch. — plural verb

When a compound subject is joined by the word *or*, the verb agrees with the subject closest to the verb.

singular subject / singular verb

plural subject — Either the (cats) or the (dog) (wakes) me up in the morning.

Either the (dog) or the (cats) (wake) me up in the morning.

singular subject / plural subject / plural verb

LOOK OUT!

Sometimes the subject comes after the verb.

• There are many vegetables in the salad.

• Here is my mother.

There and here are not subjects.

Ignore Any Extra Words

When choosing the correct verb, keep your eye on the subject of the sentence. Words that come between a subject and its verb do not affect the subject-verb agreement.

The price for those shoes is too high!

The flowers in that vase are wilting.

YOUR TURN!

Are We All in Agreement?

Fill in the blank with the correct verb form for each compound subject.

• Paul and his brothers _____ to the same school.
  (go/goes)

• Either Paul's brothers or his sister _____ in the newspaper.
  (bring/brings)

• Either Paul's sister or his brothers _____ in the newspaper.
  (bring/brings)

• The boys and their dog _____ around the block every evening.
  (walk/walks)

• Lauren or her sisters _____ every race they enter.
  (win/wins)

• Cats or a dog _____ allowed in that apartment building.
  (is/are)

Collective Nouns

Collective nouns name groups of things.

army	committee	gang
audience	crowd	group
band	faculty	jury
class	family	team

In general, use a singular verb when the action refers to the group as a single unit, and a plural verb when members of the group are acting as individuals.

singular verb

collective noun The (jury) (finds) the defendant guilty.

The (jury) (live) in different parts of the city.

plural verb

The action of the jury as a group is being described in the first sentence. The people of the jury worked together to come up with the same verdict. The second sentence refers to the individual members of the jury, who live in different places. Whenever you aren't sure about a collective noun, ask yourself whether the sentence is about the group as a whole or if it is about the individual people or things that make up the collective noun.

Try rewriting the sentence without a collective noun.

Members of the jury live in different parts of the city.

Some collective nouns agree only with plural verbs.

plural verb

collective noun The (police) (are) working with the community on unsolved crimes. *correct*

singular verb

The (police) (is) working with the community on unsolved crimes. *incorrect*

plural verb

collective noun The (elderly) (need) special services. *correct*

The (elderly) (needs) special services. *incorrect*

singular verb

Animal Groups

Some common collective nouns are animal group names. Here are a few.

an army of ants

a flock of sheep

a gaggle of geese

a herd of buffalo

a litter of kittens

a pod of dolphins

a pride of lions

a school of fish

a swarm of bees

a tribe of monkeys

a pack of wolves

AGREEMENT

Matching Pronouns and Antecedents

The word a pronoun stands in for is called its **antecedent.**
The antecedent usually is mentioned before the pronoun is used.

antecedent — (My parents) joined a health club. Now (they) get more exercise. — *pronoun*

A pronoun must agree with its antecedent. So, if the antecedent is plural, the pronoun should be plural too.

The **children** played soccer. ▶ **They** played soccer.

Pronouns must also be the same **gender** as their antecedent. *Gender* refers to whether a word is masculine (boy, man, he, him, his) or feminine (girl, woman, she, her, hers).

feminine antecedent — (Grace) scored a goal. ▶ (She) scored a goal. — *feminine pronoun*

masculine antecedent — (Gus) scored a goal. ▶ (He) scored a goal. — *masculine pronoun*

Here are the singular and plural forms of common pronouns.

Subject Pronouns		Object Pronouns	
SINGULAR	PLURAL	SINGULAR	PLURAL
I	we	me	us
you	you	you	you
he, she, it	they	him, her, it	them

Possessive		Reflexive Pronouns	
SINGULAR	PLURAL	SINGULAR	PLURAL
my, mine	our, ours	myself	ourselves
your, yours	your, yours	yourself	yourselves
his, hers, its	their, theirs	himself, herself, itself	themselves

Notice that only some singular forms are either masculine or feminine.

Which Pronouns Work?

> Write at least two pronouns you could use for each of the antecedents.
> Use the chart on page 66 if you need help.

Mr. Smith _____

a book _____

grandparents _____

Mrs. McGee _____

flowers _____

a mouse _____

brothers _____

His or Hers? What If the Gender Is Unclear?

Sometimes you don't know if an antecedent is masculine or feminine.

Suppose your teacher says:

"Any student who forgets her homework gets a demerit."

This is fine if all the students are girls, but not if there are boys and girls in the same class.

The teacher could say:

"Any student who forgets his or her homework gets a demerit."

Another option is to make the antecedent plural and avoid the gender issue altogether:

"Students who forget their homework get a demerit."

LOOK OUT!

One common mistake is to use the word *they* or *their* when the gender of the antecedent isn't clear.

- "Any student **who forgets** his or her **homework gets a demerit."** correct
- "Any student who forgets **their homework gets a demerit."** incorrect

Using a plural pronoun for a singular antecedent is always incorrect.

NEGATIVES

Creating Contractions

The words *no, not, none,* and *never* are called **negatives.**

> There were **not** enough characters in the play to give everyone a part.

> The director needs **no** more actors.

> Glen wanted a part, but there were **none** left.

Contractions such as *don't* and *can't* are also negatives. In a negative contraction, **-n't** stands for the adverb *not.*

can + **not** = can't

> Lee Ann **can't** rehearse with us.

is + **not** = isn't

> It **isn't** unusual to be nervous

Some Common Negative Contractions

aren't	don't	shouldn't
can't	hasn't	wasn't
couldn't	haven't	weren't
didn't	isn't	won't
doesn't	mustn't	wouldn't

YOUR TURN!

Shouldn't He Study His Lines?

Read the sentences below. Circle all the negatives. Don't forget to circle the negative contractions as well.

Gary and Lenny are trying out for the same part in the class play. One boy isn't going to get the part. Nobody knows whom the director will choose. Gary has never been in a play before. He does not want to make a mistake while he is trying out. Lenny hopes that he won't be disappointed, but he hasn't studied his lines. The director will not be happy about that!

Say "No! No!" to Double Negatives

In general, try to avoid using more than one negative in a sentence. Just as in math, two negatives cancel each other out. These two sentences have similar meanings.

If it isn't broken, don't fix it.

If it is broken, fix it.

The first sentence has two negatives, or a **double negative,** in it. The second sentence has no negatives. They have similar meanings. Now look at this sentence:

I didn't do nothing!

If you **didn't** do **nothing**, then you *did* do *something,* and it sounds like it could get you in big trouble. So, if you want to plead innocent, try:

I didn't do anything!

Don't Fall into the Double Negative Trap!

> Choose and (circle) the correct word to avoid a double negative.

The play that our class is putting on is about a jewel thief and a detective. The jewel thief is (anyone/no one) you would want to know. He is dishonest and mean. The detective doesn't seem to have (any/no) luck in her pursuit of the thief. The thief never leaves clues when he robs a mansion. He hasn't even left behind (no/one) fingerprint. At first, the detective doesn't have (no/any) luck, but then the jewel thief makes a mistake. He wants to break into a safe, but he can't find (no/any) gloves (anywhere/nowhere)!

Warning: Double Negatives Ahead

> Each of the sentences below desperately needs your help! Rewrite each one to remove the double negative.

I don't want nothing.

I don't want anything.

Don't never do that again!

_____

She can't have no more pie.

_____

I don't get no respect.

_____

I didn't break no one's window.

_____

I can't write no more.

_____

NUMBERS

Writing with Numbers

When you do your math homework or write a science lab report, you use numerals.

$$2 + 2 = 4$$

But when you are writing a paragraph in your English class, spell out number words.

Two plus two equals four.

Even expert writers do not always agree about when and how to write with numbers. But magazine, newspaper, and book editors will pick one style and stick with it. Here are the two most common styles used when writing with numbers.

> **PAY ATTENTION**
> Next time you are reading a book, newspaper, or magazine article, pay special attention to how the writer uses numerals and number words.

Style #1: Spell out whole numbers from zero through nine.

Style #2: Spell out whole numbers from zero through one hundred.

It doesn't matter which rule you choose to follow as long as you are consistent.

Our two cats eat nine pounds of food a month. *correct*	Our two cats eat 9 pounds of food a month. *incorrect*
My neighbor has 12 cats, and they eat 14 pounds of food a month. *correct*	Our 2 cats eat 9 pounds of food a month. *incorrect*
My neighbor has twelve cats, and they eat fourteen pounds of food a month. *correct*	My neighbor has 12 cats, and they eat fourteen pounds of food a month. *incorrect*

No matter which style you follow, most numbers higher than one hundred do not need to be spelled out.

Two new movie theaters can seat exactly 512 people. *correct*

I counted 183 pencils, but only four are sharpened. *correct*

What You Are Writing Matters

These writing-with-numbers rules apply when you are writing a story, an essay, or a newspaper article but not when you are writing a lab report for science class, a list, or a recipe. That's why there are numerals in *Style #1* and *Style #2* above. The numerals are part of a numbered list and are not really part of a sentence.

Big Numbers

When following either of these styles, you usually spell out large round numbers such as:

five hundred (500)

six thousand (6,000)

one million (1,000,000)

Use numerals for other large numbers.

Paul counted 1,346 motorcycles during a cross-country road trip with his family. *correct*

Paul guessed that they passed six thousand more while he was asleep in the back seat. *correct*

Here are some common numbers spelled out.

Numeral	Spelled Out
1	one
11	eleven
14	fourteen
16	sixteen
21	twenty-one
32	thirty-two
50	fifty
600	six hundred
2,000,000	two million

Who's on First?

Ordinal numbers, like first, third, and 25th, show that things are ranked in some way. Here are some ordinal numbers.

Ordinal Number	Ordinal Number Word
1st	first
11th	eleventh
14th	fourteenth
25th	twenty-fifth
32nd	thirty-second
43rd	forty-third
50th	fiftieth
600th	six hundredth

When you are writing, spell out ordinals that are only one word long. Use ordinal numbers when the number is more than one word.

Henrietta came in first in the race.

George placed third.

Karen and Camille were 33rd and 34th.

LOOK OUT!

Notice that some number words use a hyphen.

- twenty-one
- thirty-two
- fifty-seven
- one hundred ninety-six

Spelling Counts!

Even though *four* is spelled with a *u, forty* is not.

4 ▸ four

14 ▸ fourteen

40 ▸ forty

71

NUMBERS

Be Careful with Beginnings

A sentence should never begin with a numeral.

Two heads are better than one. correct

20 shoes are better than 19. incorrect

Sometimes it is better to rewrite a sentence so the number is not at the beginning, instead of spelling it out.

Three hundred fourteen is my favorite number. correct

My favorite number is 314. correct (better)

Addresses and Dates

Always use numerals with addresses, P.O. boxes, apartment numbers, and ZIP codes.

> **The babysitter lives at 432 Turf Valley Drive.**
>
> **Please send the check to:**
>
> **Mrs. Deborah Smith**
> **1701 Main Street, Apt. #4**
> **Grammartown, FL 33101**

When writing dates, always use numerals for the year. When a specific date is mentioned, use numerals for the date and the year. If you are referring to a date without the month or year, spell out the date.

> **I think 2015 is going to be a great year.**
>
> **The package will be delivered by February 2, 2014.**
>
> **Dad made sure to order the Thanksgiving pies by November 10.**
>
> **My birthday is on the fifth.**

Use numerals when you refer to a series of page numbers.

> **For tonight's homework, I must read pages 9–17.**

YOUR TURN!

Number Know-How

Fill in the blanks in these sentences using either the numeral or the number word.

- Dogs have _____ legs, but people have only _____.
  (4/four)   (2/two)

- Thomas was absent _____ days over a period of _____ months.
  (8/eight)   (3/three)

- Kylie watched _____ airplanes take off while she waited _____ minutes
  (60/sixty)   (30/thirty)
  for her flight to board.

- Harry visited _____ websites to find the information he needed to
  (17/seventeen)
  answer the _____ social studies questions.
  (20/twenty)

- My family has _____ dog, _____ cats, _____ birds, and _____
  (1/one)   (3/three)   (2/two)   (23/twenty-three)
  tropical fish.

Fractions

When completing math problems, use numerals to make up fractions. When writing, spell out simple fractions. To properly write out fractions, you'll need to use a hyphen.

> Only **one-tenth** of the eligible voters cast a ballot in yesterday's town elections.

> **Two-thirds** of Hallie's kittens had already moved to new homes.

Here are some common fractions spelled out.

Fraction	Fraction Spelled Out
1/2	one-half
1/3	one-third
1/4	one-fourth (or "one-quarter")
1/6	one-sixth
1/10	one-tenth
2/3	two-thirds
3/5	three-fifths

Use Your Imagination . . . and Your Knowledge of Numbers

YOUR TURN!

Write captions for these pictures using numerals and number words.

_____

_____

_____

_____

_____

_____

_____

_____

_____

TITLES

Tackling Titles

Titles are names that help us identify a specific book, movie, poem, song, play, magazine, painting or other artwork, and many other things.

Important words in a title begin with a capital letter. The first word, even if that word is *a* or *the,* begins with a capital. In addition, titles of books, movies, and other works that stand alone should be <u>underlined</u> when written by hand, or typed using an *italic* font.

My book report is about <u>Diary of a Wimpy Kid.</u>

Molly's parents read *The Wind in the Willows* to her at bedtime.

Da Vinci's *Mona Lisa* is the most famous painting in the world.

My parents get the *New York Times* delivered to our house on Sundays.

Selena Gomez appeared in *Barney & Friends,* but it was the *Wizards of Waverly Place* that really made her famous.

Titles for these should be underlined or appear in italics:

- books
- movies
- TV series
- magazines
- plays
- CDs (albums)
- newspapers
- artworks

LOOK OUT!
The Bible and other religious books are capitalized but do not appear in italics.

People Can Have Titles Too

Some titles are important jobs in our government. Titles begin with a capital letter when they come right before the person's name.

As part of her duties, Secretary of State Hillary Clinton traveled all around the world.

George W. Bush defeated Governor Ann Richards in 1994.

Some titles refer to a person's rank in the military.

A portrait of Captain John Smith appears on an old map of New England.

Historians agree that General Ulysses S. Grant won the Civil War for the Union.

Titles are often lowercase when they are not used with the person's name.

Hillary Clinton served as secretary of state for four years.

Ann Richards was a Texas state treasurer before she became governor.

Italics vs. Quotation Marks

Titles of songs and poems should be written with quotation marks around them. This goes for short stories and newspaper and magazine articles as well.

Nia likes to listen to **"What Makes You Beautiful"** when she works out.

Robert Frost wrote many great poems, but my favorite is **"The Road Not Taken."**

After reading **"Building a Worm Box"** in his grandmother's gardening magazine, Reg decided to make one himself.

How can you remember which titles take "quotation marks" and which are underlined or in *italics*? Think bigger and smaller. Titles of bigger (or longer) works are underlined or set in *italics*. Titles of smaller (or shorter) works get "quotation marks" instead. Here's how this works:

- A book of poems includes many poems. When you refer to the title of the poetry book, it should be in italics or underlined. Poems are smaller. Their titles get quotation marks instead.

- The title of a magazine (like *Time* or *People*) should be in italics or underlined. Titles of articles that appear in a magazine get quotation marks.

- The title of a CD should be in italics or underlined. Song titles get quotation marks.

YOUR TURN!

Title Tune-Up

This paragraph includes many titles. Underline the "bigger" titles, and put quotation marks around the "smaller" titles.

One Direction's first single, What Makes You Beautiful, was released in the U.K. in September 2011 and shot to the top of the charts. The group released its first U.S. album, Up All Night, on March 13, 2012. Billboard magazine reported that the album was an immediate hit. Later, the group was on the TV show iCarly. The singers made a special appearance on the episode called iGo One Direction. After releasing the album Take Me Home, in November 2012, they set out on a massive world tour, traveling through Europe, Australia, and North America.

ABBREVIATIONS

BLVD.

Acing Abbreviations

An **abbreviation** is a shortened form of a word. We use abbreviations when we write the names of cities, states, and even our own country (U.S.).

Here are some city names that are often abbreviated.

St. Louis   Ft. Myers

St. Paul   Washington, D.C.

Mt. Airy

When writing a state name in an address, use two capital letters and no periods. Here are the abbreviations for the U.S. states.

D.C. stands for the District of Columbia.

Streets and Roads

We use these abbreviations for writing addresses.

Ave. ▶ Avenue

Blvd. ▶ Boulevard

Dr. ▶ Drive

Ln. ▶ Lane

Pkwy. ▶ Parkway

Rd. ▶ Road

St. ▶ Street

Sq. ▶ Square

State Names and Abbreviations

Alabama ▶ AL
Alaska ▶ AK
Arizona ▶ AZ
Arkansas ▶ AR
California ▶ CA
Colorado ▶ CO
Connecticut ▶ CT
Delaware ▶ DE
Florida ▶ FL
Georgia ▶ GA
Hawaii ▶ HI
Idaho ▶ ID
Illinois ▶ IL
Indiana ▶ IN
Iowa ▶ IA
Kansas ▶ KS
Kentucky ▶ KY

State Names and Abbreviations

Louisiana ▶ LA
Maine ▶ ME
Maryland ▶ MD
Massachusetts ▶ MA
Michigan ▶ MI
Minnesota ▶ MN
Mississippi ▶ MS
Missouri ▶ MO
Montana ▶ MT
Nebraska ▶ NE
Nevada ▶ NV
New Hampshire ▶ NH
New Jersey ▶ NJ
New Mexico ▶ NM
New York ▶ NY
North Carolina ▶ NC
North Dakota ▶ ND

State Names and Abbreviations

Ohio ▶ OH
Oklahoma ▶ OK
Oregon ▶ OR
Pennsylvania ▶ PA
Rhode Island ▶ RI
South Carolina ▶ SC
South Dakota ▶ SD
Tennessee ▶ TN
Texas ▶ TX
Utah ▶ UT
Vermont ▶ VT
Virginia ▶ VA
Washington ▶ WA
West Virginia ▶ WV
Wisconsin ▶ WI
Wyoming ▶ WY

Abbreviations with a Person's Name

You already know some common abbreviations that go in front of a person's name. In fact, you probably use them every day when you address a teacher, parent, or doctor.

Mrs.

Ms.

Mr.

Dr.

The title *Ms.* does not specify if a woman is single or married and can be used instead of either Miss or Mrs.

An abbreviation may be added after a person's name if his father or son has the exact same name.

Jr.

Sr.

Titles can be written as abbreviations. When abbreviating a person's title, capitalize the first letter of the title and put a period at the end of the abbreviation.

LOOK OUT!

The title *Miss* is not an abbreviation, so do not put a period at the end.

Academic Degrees

We use abbreviations after people's names to tell more about them. There are many abbreviations for degrees earned from colleges and universities. Here are a few.

BA and **BS** stand for bachelor of arts and bachelor of science. These abbreviations mean that a person graduated from an undergraduate college program.

MA and **MS** mean master of arts and master of science. These abbreviations mean that a person graduated from graduate school.

MD means that someone is a medical doctor.

MFA stands for master of fine arts. This means a person completed a graduate school program in painting, film, photography, theater, music, writing, or another artistic field of study.

DDS stands for doctor of dental surgery. A person with DDS after his or her name is a dentist.

JD means *juris doctor*, or doctor of law. A person with JD after his or her name is a lawyer.

MBA means master of business administration.

PhD stands for *philosophiae doctor*, or doctor of philosophy. It is the highest degree awarded for graduate study.

Title	Abbreviation
Doctor	Dr.
Captain	Capt.
Colonel	Col.
General	Gen.
Lieutenant	Lt.
Lieutenant Colonel	Lt. Col.
Professor	Prof.
Representative	Rep.
Reverend	Rev.
Sergeant	Sgt.
Senator	Sen.

ABBREVIATIONS

Days and Dates

There are abbreviations for the days of the week and the months of the year.

They begin with a capital letter and end with a period. Note: May, June, and July are not usually abbreviated.

Mon.	Jan.
Tue. (or Tues.)	Feb.
Wed.	Mar.
Thur. (or Thurs.)	Apr.
Fri.	Aug.
Sat.	Sept.
Sun.	Oct.
	Nov.
	Dec.

Telling Time

The commonly used abbreviations a.m. and p.m. come from the Latin words *ante meridiem* and *post meridiem*, which mean "before noon" and "after noon." Most people use these abbreviations without ever knowing the Latin words they stand for.

It's 8 p.m.

Acronyms vs. Initialisms

An **acronym** is made up of the first letters of each word in a phrase. It is generally written with all capital letters and can be spoken aloud as one word. Here are a few common ones.

AIDS	NASA
EPCOT	NASCAR
FEMA	NATO

FEMA — Federal Emergency Management Agency

NATO — North Atlantic Treaty Organization

NASCAR — National Association for Stock Car Auto Racing

Initialisms are acronyms that are not usually pronounced as words. Each letter in an initialism is pronounced.

IBM	FAQ	TBA
CIA	NBA	UN

TBA — to be announced

UN — United Nations

Some words began as acronyms but are now often written in lowercase, just like most other words.

laser	scuba
radar	sonar

laser — light amplification by stimulated emission of radiation

radar — radio detection and ranging

scuba — self-contained underwater breathing apparatus

sonar — sound navigation and ranging

Shortened Search-a-Word

Using the hint box below, find and circle 20 words that are often abbreviated. The words may run forward, backward, up, down, and diagonally. Circle them all.

Y	A	W	K	R	A	P	A	S	R	X	E	I	J	A	T	I	X	A	P	R	M	C	V	E
C	L	D	N	K	G	B	L	G	Q	Z	K	L	Q	R	Z	T	O	E	M	F	I	G	C	P
E	D	W	I	E	P	E	P	V	Y	I	P	M	L	P	W	L	J	I	H	R	O	X	M	D
C	V	Z	W	E	A	R	K	A	N	S	A	S	Z	O	G	M	K	S	G	I	P	R	P	T
X	I	L	F	L	R	M	L	O	O	C	E	E	U	A	C	I	U	P	C	D	E	C	T	I
O	H	F	N	E	D	C	O	C	H	Z	R	N	O	I	V	S	N	D	I	A	T	D	I	D
U	B	C	C	H	S	O	E	A	U	X	F	A	I	E	P	S	Y	E	L	Y	Z	A	V	L
J	T	M	P	Z	S	Y	C	P	N	I	F	T	M	A	O	O	I	A	Q	U	G	I	R	O
I	N	F	I	O	I	X	L	T	Y	N	R	O	A	D	G	U	K	S	D	Z	L	O	E	A
A	O	J	T	F	H	Q	I	A	O	M	V	R	E	I	Q	R	E	R	N	S	E	D	I	E
K	V	E	E	K	Q	E	E	I	N	R	H	B	U	O	E	I	P	H	Z	B	E	K	V	G
A	E	C	U	I	R	X	M	N	H	U	A	I	F	A	P	T	E	V	H	E	Z	U	T	Z
V	M	I	S	T	E	R	B	O	A	W	R	A	O	G	T	Z	S	U	M	A	T	S	T	I
E	B	O	Y	Q	I	J	I	B	K	S	S	O	E	U	R	U	N	E	O	F	H	K	W	H
I	E	E	P	S	T	F	G	H	T	C	G	D	F	P	J	H	R	X	U	Q	C	X	L	E
J	R	V	P	X	K	I	F	E	B	I	V	U	R	C	A	N	K	D	N	I	K	A	I	O
K	L	C	K	R	E	V	Z	O	N	Q	J	E	O	Z	N	D	U	S	T	R	E	E	T	H
N	E	I	C	E	O	I	L	L	I	N	O	I	S	M	U	P	Q	M	O	T	O	I	S	N
O	N	A	F	F	N	S	R	U	Y	E	S	P	Y	U	A	Y	O	P	E	C	L	U	A	E
U	L	R	O	I	O	T	P	K	H	A	M	E	S	E	R	G	E	A	N	T	H	E	B	F
S	D	X	L	C	K	M	U	B	M	Z	H	J	E	U	Y	P	R	O	F	E	S	S	O	R
I	E	U	O	V	E	Z	L	C	O	E	I	Y	L	B	V	A	L	S	P	I	U	L	P	O
R	G	H	H	O	Q	O	Y	R	K	M	U	E	J	O	I	Z	O	X	Z	M	O	S	X	V
Z	X	C	V	F	P	L	Z	B	M	Y	O	S	N	E	S	B	A	E	X	C	A	A	E	P
S	E	Q	B	O	U	L	E	V	A	R	D	O	X	J	U	L	P	F	J	N	U	O	N	F

HINT BOX

Arkansas	Fort	Kentucky	November	Senator
Boulevard	Friday	Missouri	Parkway	Sergeant
Captain	Illinois	Mister	Professor	Street
Doctor	January	Mount	Road	Tuesday

PUNCTUATION

Some punctuation rules are easy to remember, like whether to use a period or a question mark at the end of a sentence. Other punctuation rules can be confusing, like whether to use a comma in a sentence. Is it really worth figuring out where to put a small squiggly line? Yes, it is. Read on to find out why.

END PUNCTUATION

Ending a Sentence

All sentences need end punctuation. You can end a sentence with a period, a question mark, or an exclamation point. Which type of end punctuation you choose depends on the kind of sentences you have written.

The same sentence can have different meanings when you change the end punctuation.

Statement ▶ It's time to go.

Question ▶ It's time to go?

Exclamation ▶ It's time to go!

• A **period** is the smallest punctuation mark. It's just a little round dot. Yet most sentences would not be complete without it.

> I have to go to the store.
>
> It was chilly outside, so Jess grabbed a sweater.
>
> Bananas are high in potassium.

? Is this a question? Yes, it is a question, so use a **question mark.**

> Is it time to go?
>
> Where is my jacket?
>
> Are we there yet?

LOOK OUT!

Do not use a question mark with a statement about a question. Use a period instead.

• I asked whether it's time to go.
  correct

• I asked whether it's time to go?
  incorrect

Common Question Words

Questions often begin with these words.

Who	How
What	Do
Where	Can
When	May
Why	Is

Some sentences demand immediate attention. An **exclamation point,** or exclamation mark, signals that this is no ordinary sentence.

!

Watch out!   **Look at that!**   **Help me!**

Don't overuse exclamation points!!
One is enough.

YOUR TURN!

Pick Your Punctuation

Add the correct end punctuation to each of these sentences.

- How old were you when you lost your first baby tooth_____

- Jack learned how to make a worm box in science class_____

- No one really knows what happens during time travel_____

- What is the capital of Iowa_____

- I know why you said that_____

- Emma wishes she knew why her socks keep disappearing_____

- Don't touch that wire_____

- When is our social studies project due_____

- Jane accidentally left her sweatshirt at the library_____

- Look, there's a shooting star_____

Follow the Arrows

Answer the questions in the hint boxes to find clues that will help you through this question-mark maze.

HINT #4

Follow the orange arrow if both sentences have the correct punctuation. Follow the green arrow if only one of the sentences is correct.

Mazes are more fun than puzzles.

Do you think mazes are more fun than puzzles.

HINT #2

Follow the orange arrow if this sentence should have a question mark. Follow the green arrow if it should not.

What's the big rush

HINT #3

Follow the orange arrow if the top sentence is correct. Follow the green arrow if the bottom sentence is correct.

The teacher asked me what my favorite color is?

The teacher asked me what my favorite color is.

HINT #1

Follow the orange arrow if this sentence should end with an exclamation point. Follow the green arrow if this sentence should end with a question mark.

Run for your life

START

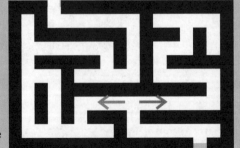

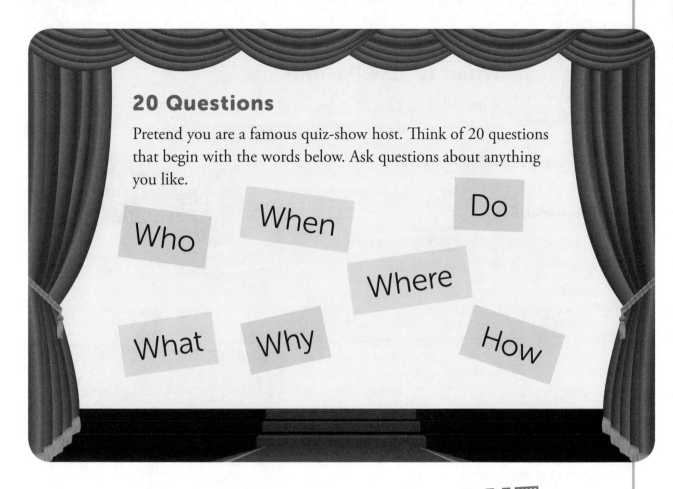

20 Questions

Pretend you are a famous quiz-show host. Think of 20 questions that begin with the words below. Ask questions about anything you like.

Who

When

Do

Where

What

Why

How

A WONDROUS PLANT

Draw a line from part of a sentence on the left to part of a sentence on the right. The end punctuation can provide hints about which words belong together. Make sure the sentences all make sense.

What is	the size of one candy sprinkle.
Its common name is	on the surface of calm, fresh water.
The plant itself is about	the smallest flower in the world?
That's	watermeal.
How much does	amazing plant!
It weighs	it weigh?
Where does	tiny!
This unusual plant floats	it live?
What an	as much as only two grains of table salt!

PERIODS

When to Use Periods

A **period** is very handy punctuation. It appears at the end of complete sentences, as well as in many other places.

Use periods after initials in a name.

> **E.B. White**
>
> **Michael J. Fox**

Periods serve as decimal points when writing out amounts of money as numerals.

> **$5.35**
>
> **$103.22**

Use periods after the abbreviations for months and days.

Jan.	**Mon.**
Oct.	**Sat.**

Use two periods with the abbreviations a.m. and p.m.

> **8 a.m.**
>
> **4 p.m.**

LOOK OUT!

If a sentence ends with an abbreviation that takes a period, do not add a second period as end punctuation.

- I woke up at 7:00 a.m. correct
- I went to bed at 9:30 p.m.. incorrect

Periods are used after many abbreviations that use uppercase and lowercase letters.

Mr.	**St.**	**Ft.**
Mrs.	**Rd.**	**Mt.**

(For more on abbreviations, see pages 76–78.)

YOUR TURN!

Use Your Eagle Eyes

> Look closely at these sentences. Find the punctuation mistake(s) in each one and correct it (them).

- My full name is Clarkson Kensington Royce, but my friends call me C.K..

- My alarm clock must be broken because it went off at 4 am.

- Mr and Mrs Hendricks just got a new dog.

- J K. Rowling is my favorite author.

- Sally counted 243 pennies for a total of $24.3.

Testing, Testing

Did you remember the rules you just learned? Read the rules below.
Circle *do* if the rule is correct. Circle *don't* if the rule is incorrect.

- You do/don't put a period after initials in a person's name.

- You do/don't have two periods at the end of a sentence.

- You do/don't end a statement about a question with a period.

- You do/don't end a question with a period.

What's Missing?

The proofreader's mark that looks like this ⊙ shows that a period is missing
and needs to be added. In the paragraph below, prove your proofreading
skills by adding in all the missing periods.

I went to my local bookstore on Saturday around 1pm to find a book for my book report. I picked out *Wonder*, by R J Palacio. The librarian, Ms Thomas, was very helpful She recommended a series of books called The Sisters Grimm, by Michael Buckley. I bought three books, which cost $3127 all together. The bookstore is on Washington St There are so many fantastic books there! You should check it out

COMMAS

When to Use Commas

A **comma** is like a divider. It sets off a word or group of words in a sentence. Unlike end punctuation, a comma appears only in the middle of a sentence, and a single sentence may need several commas to be correct.

Commas can make or break the meaning of a sentence. Think about how adding a comma to this sentence might change its meaning.

Let's eat Grandma.

Let's eat, Grandma.

Use a comma after the words *yes* and *no* or after other expressions, exclamations, and interjections at the beginning of a sentence.

Yes, I do like chocolate on my spaghetti.

Wow, that's a lot of chocolate!

Sometimes the introductory part of a sentence is more than one word.

No way, potatoes can't grow inside your ear.

It's true, mushrooms can grow inside a closet.

Are you talking to me? Some sentences include the name of the person being addressed (spoken or written to) directly. If the person's name is at the beginning of the sentence, put a comma after the name.

Jon, please pass the salt.

Kara, are you coming with us?

If the person's name is in the middle of the sentence, put commas before and after the name.

I said, Jon, please pass the salt.

Are you, Kara, coming with us?

If the person's name is at the end of the sentence, put a comma before the name.

Please pass the salt, Jon.

Are you coming with us, Kara?

Use a comma only when the person named is being addressed directly.

Jon passed the salt.

I passed the salt to Jon.

Commas with Nonessential Words or Phrases

Use commas to set off **nonessential words and phrases.** How can you tell if a word or phrase is nonessential? Just take it out of the sentence to see if the meaning of the sentence is still clear.

The test, _however_, was harder than Joey expected. — *a nonessential word*

The test was harder than Joey expected. ← *When you remove however, the sentence still makes sense.*

Notice that the nonessential words or phrases can be at the beginning, middle, or end of a sentence. At the beginning or end of a sentence, the nonessential information requires only one comma. When the nonessential information is in the middle of the sentence, it needs two commas.

Sentences with Nonessential Words and Phrases	Sentences with Nonessential Words and Phrases Removed
On several occasions, George forgot to hand in his homework.	George forgot to hand in his homework.
George, hoping for an A, did the extra-credit assignment.	George did the extra-credit assignment.
Reg refused to eat any blue foods, even blueberries.	Reg refused to eat any blue foods.

What Is an Appositive?

An **appositive** is a noun or noun phrase that renames, describes, or explains another noun right beside it. Appositives can come right after or right before the noun they describe. They can be long or short.

The largest city in Brazil is Brasília, the country's capital city.

Rio de Janiero, the second-largest city in Brazil, is home to more than six million people.

The world's biggest party, Carnival, takes place in Rio de Janeiro.

COMMAS

Commas and Clauses

Many short, simple sentences are fine without commas, but long sentences with more than one clause may need commas.

Commas and Independent Clauses

Use a comma before a coordinating conjunction when you join two independent clauses to make a compound sentence.

coordinating conjunction

> My sister likes turnips, (but) I like beets.
>
> She was late, so she missed the bus.
>
> We can go to the movies, and we can go shopping.
>
> You can have milk, or you can have juice.
>
> It was freezing out, yet the sun was shining.

Commas and Dependent Clauses

A complex sentence includes an independent clause, which can stand alone as a sentence, and a **dependent clause,** which cannot stand alone as a sentence. Use a comma when a dependent clause comes at the beginning of a complex sentence.

> Before you go to sleep, brush your teeth.
>
> If you eat breakfast, you will have more energy during the day.

You don't need a comma if the independent clause comes first.

> Brush your teeth before you go to bed.
>
> You will have more energy during the day if you eat breakfast.

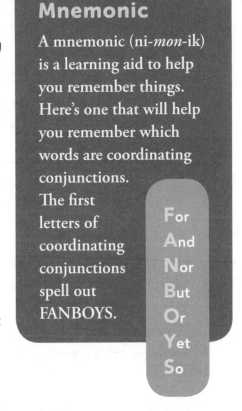

Mnemonic

A mnemonic (ni-*mon*-ik) is a learning aid to help you remember things. Here's one that will help you remember which words are coordinating conjunctions. The first letters of coordinating conjunctions spell out FANBOYS.

For
And
Nor
But
Or
Yet
So

While I brush my teeth, I think about commas.

Using Commas to Avoid Confusion

Commas can be incredibly helpful in making sentences more clear. Look at the two sentences below.

The cat said the boy likes to catch mice.

The cat, said the boy, likes to catch mice.

The first sentence would make sense if cats could talk. The second sentence uses commas to make it clear who is doing the talking.

YOUR TURN!

Comma Quest

> Some (but not all) of the sentences below need a comma. If the sentence is correct as written, leave it as is. If the sentence needs a comma, write it in.

- Mariska won first place at the science fair.

- Yuck I wish the cat would use its litter box.

- You're right the capital of South Dakota is Pierre.

- My goodness you've grown a foot and a half since I last saw you.

- Jack likes going out to eat but he only likes Chinese restaurants.

- If you say that again I'm going to scream.

- Pat went out for ice cream after the movie.

- I told Jeff to take out the trash.

- Peggy Sue wanted a good grade so she studied hard for the math test.

- Although Olga tried her best she did not win the geography bee.

- While walking to school Ingrid accidentally stepped on a caterpillar.

COMMAS

Commas with Several Items

Use commas to separate three or more items in a series.

We bought oranges, strawberries, and blueberries for the fruit salad. *correct*

We bought oranges strawberries and blueberries for the fruit salad. *incorrect*

Look at the two sentences below. How many girls went to the mall?

> **Mary Ann and I went to the mall.**

> **Mary, Ann, and I went to the mall.**

Is *Mary Ann* referring to one girl or two? A correctly placed comma can answer that question.

Serial Commas

In a list of three or more things, the comma before the conjunction (in this case, it is *and*) is called a serial comma. Some writers do not use serial commas. As long as writers are consistent, they are still correct. Using this serial comma is becoming more and more common. It is used throughout this book.

We put carrots, peas and onions in the soup.

serial comma

Mary Ann and I

Mary, Ann, and I

YOUR TURN!

Where Did All the Commas Go?

> Add commas to separate the items listed in these sentences.

- Fred bought notebooks pencils pens markers and book covers at the back-to-school sale.

- A good diet includes fruits vegetables and grains as well as high-protein foods, such as eggs meat dairy fish and chicken.

- Justin put forks knives and spoons on the table.

- Ceci found socks shoes and an old sandwich under her bed.

- Katie got a necklace a bag of candy and two books for her birthday.

More Uses of the Comma

Commas have many uses. Here are more ways to use commas correctly.

Use a comma to separate contrasting parts of a sentence.

This is my lunch, not yours.

Karin wanted eggs, not pancakes, for breakfast.

Use a comma with titles or degrees that come after a person's name.

Ruth K. James, PhD

Herbert Hicks, MD

Place a comma between the day and the date. Also, when writing out dates, use commas between the date and the year.

Kofi's birthday is Tuesday, June 18.

Taylor Swift was born on December 13, 1989.

A comma is not necessary when you write only the date, or only the month and year.

I look forward to seeing you on December 4.

The bill passed in June 2010.

Use a comma between a city and its state. If the state name is in the middle of a sentence, be sure to use two commas.

Sarah is from Columbia, Maryland.

Sarah visits Columbia, Maryland, twice a year.

Use commas when writing addresses. A comma separates the street address from the city and state. You do not need a comma to separate the state from the ZIP code.

The pet store is at 1804 St. John's Lane, Atlanta, Georgia 30304.

Irving lives at 57 Bear Mountain Drive, Apartment 3, Breckenridge, Colorado 80424.

Use commas when you address an envelope and when you write a letter.

March 21, 2013

Dear Uncle Conor,

Thank you so much for the wonderful birthday presents. Wow, they are awesome! I love to skateboard, and it was very thoughtful of you to buy me a new set of wheels. Now when my wheels get worn down, I can switch to my shiny, new set. I can't wait to see you on Thanksgiving!

Sincerely,
Bobby

Bobby Watson
326 Oakmore Lane
Chesterfield, NJ 08515

Conor Corcoran
43 Pistachio Way
Terra Bella, CA 93270

COMMAS

Do You Really Need a Comma?

Using commas often comes down to good judgment.
Look at these two sentences. Which is easier to read and
understand?

Logan walked in in his new suit.

Logan walked in, in his new suit.

Rule Reminder

1. Place a comma after certain words, phrases, and dependent clauses that appear at the beginning of a sentence.

- Yes, doing extra-credit assignments is a good way to get your grades up.
- It's true, hard work can make a difference in your grades.
- Because he completed the extra-credit assignment, George's grade average was higher.

2. Place commas before and after interrupting elements that appear in the middle of a sentence.

- George's teacher, it turns out, did the right thing.

3. Use a comma and end punctuation to enclose a tagged-on word or phrase.

- George was glad he got that A, eventually.

4. Place a comma before a coordinating conjunction joining independent clauses.

- George did the extra-credit assignment, and his teacher gave him an A.

5. Place a comma between elements in a series.

- George got an A in science, a B in social studies, and a B in gym.

The Great Comma Challenge

Show that you've mastered the art of using commas by adding one or more commas to the sentences below.

- Francie wanted a part in the play so she auditioned.

- When Francie entered the auditorium the auditions had already begun.

- My dog sleeps on a pillow barks in its sleep and wakes up hungry.

- When I was nine and my sister was a baby I helped her get dressed.

- The sun set in the western sky and the full moon rose in the east.

- Jack was a self-respecting intelligent teenager.

- Rebecca doesn't like speaking in front of a group even her classmates.

- As the soccer ball was flying toward the goal Jimmy tried to block it.

- It would help you know if you said you were sorry.

- If everyone recycled more we might not need a new landfill.

Going Postal

Write a postcard to yourself. Remember to write today's date at the top. Fill in your address. Use periods for abbreviations and commas to separate parts of the date and address.

POSTCARD

PLACE
STAMP
HERE

FOR ADDRESS ONLY

COLONS

When to Use Colons

A **colon** looks like two dots stacked one on top of the other.
Use a colon to introduce a list after an independent clause.

independent clause

> I found everything I needed at the store: pencils, notebook paper, and a yellow highlighter.

Even when you use a colon before a list, don't forget to use commas to separate items in the list. Look at the sentences below. Notice that the information can be conveyed with or without a colon.

With a Colon	Without a Colon
Mom puts these vegetables in her special soup: potatoes, carrots, onions, and garlic.	Mom makes a special soup with potatoes, carrots, onions, and garlic.
Judy has homework due tomorrow: an essay for English class, a lab report for science, and a worksheet on percentages for math.	Judy's homework, which is due tomorrow, includes an essay for English class, a lab report for science, and a worksheet on percentages for math.

LOOK OUT!

Make sure the first part of the sentence, before the colon, could make sense as a sentence. If it cannot stand on its own, then using a colon is not correct.

• Mom puts: potatoes, carrots, onions, and garlic in her special soup. incorrect

Mom puts is not an independent clause. It does not make sense on its own.

YOUR TURN!

X Marks the Spot

Some of these sentences use a colon correctly. Others do not. Make a ✓ after the ones that are correct. Draw a big ✗ after the ones that are incorrect.

- Paul collects stamps and coins: from many other countries.

- Max and his class were studying human biology in science class, including: the digestive system, the nervous system, and the brain.

- These boys made the basketball team: Luke, Ethan, Kevin, Kyle, Andrew, Gus, Michael, and Logan.

- Camp Pocahontas encourages campers to participate in all the activities offered: horseback riding, swimming, canoeing, crafts, ball sports, and archery.

- Some personality traits are helpful: when dealing with difficult people, patience, empathy, compassion, and a good sense of humor.

Use a colon to introduce an idea or an example.

The students agreed: Mr. Amend was their favorite teacher.

There is one thing you need to know about Mr. Amend: he is tough but fair.

Colons separate the number of hours from minutes when you write the time.

4:18 a.m.

3:45 p.m.

In titles, colons separate titles from subtitles.

Brothers at Bat: The True Story of an Amazing All-Brother Baseball Team

Sit-In: How Four Friends Stood Up by Sitting Down

Show Off Your Skills

Add colons, commas, and periods to these sentences so they are correctly punctuated.

- Claire made the following for the school bake sale an apple tart brownies a sheet cake with lemon frosting and a dozen cupcakes

- Gina forgot to set her alarm clock overslept and was late for work

- Marnie likes only three flavors of ice cream vanilla strawberry and chocolate

- There are many places to go skiing near Brattleboro Vermont

- Amanda has four sisters Brianna Mychaela Rhonda and Ashley

- Al and Tony argued yesterday but today they are back to being best friends

- Three teachers were out today with the flu Mr Meek Mrs Ferland and Mr Harrison

- Today's lunch options are pizza chicken nuggets fruit and salad

- Anton remembered all the state capitals except for three Rhode Island New Jersey and New Mexico

SEMICOLONS

LOOK OUT!

If the independent clauses are not related, do not use a semicolon to make them into one sentence.
• It was Sunday; my name is Josianne. incorrect

When to Use Semicolons

A **semicolon** looks like a dot on top of a comma. Use a semicolon to join two related independent clauses.

> **I have gym class right now; Corey has art.**

> **It was Sunday; we slept late.**

The sentence above could also be written in other ways.

> **It was Sunday. We slept late.**

> **It was Sunday, so we slept late.**

Use a semicolon before certain connecting words and phrases that join independent clauses in a compound sentence. Put a comma after the connecting word or phrase and before the second independent clause.

> **It was Sunday; nevertheless, we were all up at dawn.**

> **Greg left his house early; therefore, he made it to school on time.**

Use a semicolon when you have a list of phrases or clauses that already have commas in them.

> **I made a sandwich with cream cheese, pepperoni, and jelly; a smoothie with bananas, yogurt, and orange juice; and a sundae with ice cream, hot fudge sauce, and gummy bears.**

> **This summer, I went to London, England; Paris, France; Seville, Spain; and Lisbon, Portugal.**

YOUR TURN!

Match and Join

Draw lines between related sentences. Then write new sentences for each pair using a semicolon.

Grapes were on sale at the supermarket.

Fred was having a party Friday night.

Lisa felt sick during second period.

Patrick lives far away.

Daylight saving time started yesterday.

It snowed heavily last night.

He bought chips and salsa.

It takes him an hour to get to school.

School was canceled.

She went to the nurse's office.

Mom bought two bags.

We set our clocks ahead one hour.

_____

_____

_____

_____

Cool Connectors

Join the sentence pairs below into a single sentence that uses a semicolon and one of the connecting words or phrases from the Word List. Don't forget to use a comma before the second independent clause.

WORD LIST

as a result

certainly

consequently

eventually

finally

however

nevertheless

otherwise

Paulette woke up in the middle of the night.
She fell back asleep.

_____

_____

Russell forgot the combination.
He could not open his locker.

_____

_____

Johnnie forgot to water the plant.
It died.

_____

_____

The man had an alibi.
The jury still found him guilty.

_____

_____

Kim liked peanut butter.
She ate the entire jar in one sitting.

_____

_____

Kylie wanted a puppy.
Her parents decided to adopt a kitten.

_____

_____

The trash was beginning to stink.
Trevor put it in the Dumpster.

_____

PARENTHESES

When to Use Parentheses

Parentheses enclose information that is related but also separate from the rest of the text.

This is the singular form of the word.

(
One parenthesis

( )
Two parentheses

This is the plural form of the word.

Parentheses can enclose extra information, such as an example, a comment, an addition, or an explanation. The same information can often be written correctly using commas or dashes (see page 114) instead of parentheses.

Adding Extra Information with Parentheses	Adding Extra Information with Commas or Dashes
Today's homework (two pages of math and a science lab) took me three hours.	Today's homework, two pages of math and a science lab, took me three hours.
Aunt Corina loves telling stories (whether they are true or not) at family reunions.	Aunt Corina loves telling stories—whether they are true or not—at family reunions.

Whether you use parentheses, dashes, or commas in cases like these is up to you. All are grammatically correct. Using parentheses instead of commas or dashes tells your readers that you think the enclosed information is not really so important.

Parentheses are also used to add dates in text.

Benjamin Franklin (1706-1790) was the most famous American of his time. He was a great leader during the American Revolution (1775-1783).

Acronyms and abbreviations often appear in parentheses immediately following the full name or phrase that they stand for.

World War I (WWI) was a global war centered in Europe.

Some scientists at the National Oceanic and Atmospheric Administration (NOAA) study the weather.

Introducing Abbreviations

After the abbreviation or acronym has been introduced in parentheses, it can be used in the text without parentheses.

World War I (WWI) was a global war centered in Europe. General John J. Pershing was probably the most famous WWI general.

Use parentheses if a noun might be singular or plural.

We do not know the identity of the person(s) responsible for breaking the window.

Correct the mistake(s) in each sentence.

Notice that the second sentence is written so as to avoid giving away whether a sentence has one or more mistakes.

Use a single, closed parenthesis or parentheses with letters or numbers that label items in a list or sentence. Parentheses will often appear in multiple-choice quizzes.

In a recent study, which animals were described as "unusual pets"?

a) iguanas

b) tarantulas

c) ferrets

d) all of the above

You don't need to be an adult to start a business, but you do need (1) an innovative idea, (2) a business plan and budget, and (3) potential customers.

Parentheses with Other Punctuation

Parentheses can sometimes be used instead of commas but not in addition to commas. Do not use commas immediately before parentheses.

The entire hockey team (except the goalie) practiced slapshots. correct

The entire hockey team, (except the goalie) practiced slapshots. incorrect

The entire hockey team, (except the goalie), practiced slapshots. incorrect

Commas can be used after parentheses in a compound sentence.

Jules hated animals (except for his sister's monkey), but he always liked to go to the zoo.

Sometimes parentheses come at the end of a sentence. The end punctuation comes *after* the parenthesis when what is inside the parentheses is *not* a complete sentence.

He finally called (after I threatened to kidnap his cat).

When parentheses surround a complete sentence, put the end punctuation *inside* the parentheses.

That website about dinosaurs has the best illustrations. (I e-mailed you the link yesterday.)

If parentheses surround a complete question or exclamation, use end punctuation inside the parentheses.

The Halloween dance (I'm going! Are you?) is tomorrow.

PARENTHESES

YOUR TURN!

Insert a Thought

Rewrite each sentence pair as one sentence with the second idea in parentheses. There may be more than one correct way to do this.

- The school play is tonight and tomorrow. It is a dinner-theater production of *The Wizard of Oz*.

The school play (a dinner-theater production of The Wizard of Oz) is tonight and tomorrow.

- Lois Lane is a comic-book character. Lois Lane is Superman's girlfriend.

- I have an aunt who lives in Poughkeepsie. Her name is Agatha.

- There is a poem about Paul Revere. The poem was written by someone famous.

- One of the mugs is chipped. It is the one with the pink turtle.

A Punctuation Mystery

Help! The punctuation marks in the sentences below have gone haywire. Some are missing, and some are incorrect. Can you find all the mistakes?

- Koo and her husband own a farm: they grow vegetables.
- Kathleen put tomatoes; they were organic; on her sandwich.
- Alstead New Hampshire is a small town but it does have its own middle school.
- Only one student I think it was Felicity got a perfect score on the math test.

- The public library has a young adult section that's where you can find books by Rick Riordan and Scott Westerfeld.
- John forgot his gym clothes so his mother dropped off his shorts socks and sneakers during lunch.
- Lou's parents are both doctors, they work at the same hospital in downtown Cleveland.

The Great Punctuation Race

These punctuation marks have been separated from the sentences where they belong. Follow the paths that will bring them back together again.

,

.

;

)

There was a fly in the soup

The waiter was embarrassed he apologized.

The waiter brought another bowl of soup to the table and he apologized again.

The chef (wearing a tall white hat came out of the kitchen to make sure everyone was happy.

QUOTATION MARKS

When to Use Quotation Marks

A direct quote (or quotation) repeats the exact words a person said or wrote.

> "I forgot my homework," Jayden said nervously.
>
> "Just bring it in tomorrow," his teacher said.
>
> The lunch lady asked Paula, "Which would you like?"
>
> "I'll have the pizza," Paula said politely.

Do not use quotation marks for a statement about what someone said (indirect quote).

> Jayden told his teacher that he forgot his homework.
>
> His teacher said he could bring it in tomorrow.

Use quotation marks to set off the titles of songs and poems, and articles from magazines.

> Michael Jackson's song "Thriller" was a big hit when my parents were young.
>
> My little sister can recite all the words to "Humpty Dumpty."

Use quotation marks when you want to show you are using a word in an unusual way. You might be calling out the word to provide its definition or to refer to the word itself. You can also set the words apart by putting them in *italics* (as we do in this book).

> Baby Katie can't say "milk" yet.
>
> Many people don't know when to use "further" instead of "farther."

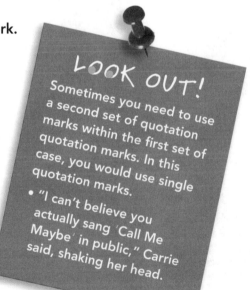

LOOK OUT!

Sometimes you need to use a second set of quotation marks within the first set of quotation marks. In this case, you would use single quotation marks.

- "I can't believe you actually sang 'Call Me Maybe' in public," Carrie said, shaking her head.

Quotation Marks and Other Punctuation

Use a comma inside the closing quotation mark when a direct quote does not end the sentence.

"Don't touch my pet rattlesnake," Kyle cautioned.

Use a comma after the introduction to a direct quote that comes at the end of a sentence.

Kyle cautioned, "Don't touch my pet rattlesnake."

When the quotation is split, you will need a comma before and after the introduction. Remember to begin the second part of the quotation with a lowercase letter if it's part of the same sentence.

"Don't touch my pet rattlesnake," Kyle cautioned, "or it might bite you."

Use a question mark inside the closing quotation mark if the quote is a direct question.

"Did you touch my pet rattlesnake?" Kyle asked suspiciously.

The period for end punctuation goes inside the quotation marks when the quotation comes at the end of the sentence.

Some would argue that Poe's most famous poem is "The Raven."

LOOK OUT!

Don't double up end punctuation even if it sometimes seems correct to do so.

- She asked, "What time is it?" correct
- She asked, "What time is it?". incorrect

YOUR TURN!

Quotation Fixer-Uppers

Each of these sentences has at least one punctuation mistake. Can you find them all? Circle the mistakes and correct them.

- "Benjamin Franklin" our teacher explained "was one of the Founding Fathers of our country."

- "That's me in the picture", she said.

- My grandparents have an old recording of Frank Sinatra singing 'My Way'.

- Aunt Harriet asked me, to "pick up her mail" while she's out of town.

- Did you take out the trash" Dad asked?

- The captain said "I hope you don't get seasick" and handed me a bucket just in case.

APOSTROPHES

When to Use Apostrophes

Apostrophes pop up in **contractions** and **possessives.**

A **possessive** noun tells who owns something. A **contraction** is a shortened version of two words with an apostrophe in place of the missing letter or letters. For more on possessives and contractions, see pages 12 and 68.

POSSESSIVE NOUNS	CONTRACTIONS WITH THE VERB *TO BE*	CONTRACTIONS WITH THE WORD *NOT*
John's	I'm	can't
Sheila's	you're	don't
my parents'	he's	won't
the dog's	she's	shouldn't
Aunt Nancy's	it's	couldn't
	they're	haven't

LOOK OUT!

If two or more people own the same thing, only the last person in the list has the 's.

• Bill and Bob's room had twin beds.

If two or more people own different things, all are possessive.

• The king's and queen's crowns were made of gold.

Apostrophes and Years

Use an apostrophe when you abbreviate a year. Make sure the apostrophe faces the correct direction.

She learned to drive during the summer of '99. *correct*

She learned to drive during the summer of '99. *incorrect*

Many people often misuse apostrophes when they refer to decades or centuries. An apostrophe is not necessary when you write decades as numerals. You can also spell out the word for the decade or century.

I love to dance to 80s music. *correct*

I love to dance to eighties music. *correct*

I love to dance to 80's music. *incorrect*

We love the 80s!

YOUR TURN!

Whose Is This?

The sentences below include possessive nouns and contractions, but the writer forgot to include the apostrophes. Circle the possessive nouns and contractions, and add the apostrophes.

- Mom found my brothers baseball mitt under the bed.

- I cant do my homework without my textbook.

- Olga found her mothers car keys in the refrigerator.

- Hes very sorry he broke your window.

- Ned stayed overnight at Brians house.

- Most toddlers dont know how to tie their shoes.

- Grandmas recipe uses buttermilk instead of sour cream.

ELLIPSES

When to Use Ellipses

Ellipses look like three dots in a row. They have two common uses: to show where something unnecessary was left out of a quotation enclosed in quotation marks, and to show a pause or slow down in thought or speech.

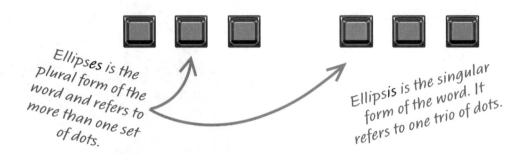

Ellipses is the plural form of the word and refers to more than one set of dots.

Ellipsis is the singular form of the word. It refers to one trio of dots.

An ellipsis shows where unnecessary text was left out of a direct quotation enclosed in quotation marks.

> "The recent crisis . . . was resolved peacefully."

> The administrator said, "If snow plows cannot clear all of the main roads . . . by 5 a.m., then we will have a snow day."

An ellipsis is not generally used at the beginning of a quotation, even if the words or phrases being quoted come from the middle of a longer quotation.

> "Tomorrow's weather is forecast to be much like it was today." *correct*

> ". . . Tomorrow's weather is forecast to be much like it was today." *incorrect*

Sometimes writers want to use only part of a long quotation. Ellipses show where parts of the quotation were left out. Ellipses can stand for one word or entire paragraphs of missing text. You often see this punctuation on the back covers of books when publishers quote favorable reviews.

> "Delightful . . . a masterpiece . . . impossible to put down . . . you'll laugh, you'll cry, you'll wish it would never end."

> "Informative and hilarious . . . A great read."

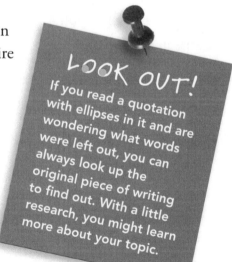

LOOK OUT!
If you read a quotation with ellipses in it and are wondering what words were left out, you can always look up the original piece of writing to find out. With a little research, you might learn more about your topic.

An ellipsis can be used to show that a sentence trails off.

Terrified of what he might find, Ken inched toward the door . . .

Cristina thought she knew where her passport was, but just to be sure . . .

Ellipses are sometimes called suspension points. A writer can use them to show that someone is pausing or slowing down in thoughts or speech.

"But, wait . . . but . . . how . . . oh, my," stammered Doug.

Kendra and Sandy got together on Sunday. They went to the park and talked and talked . . . and talked some more.

Ellipses Should NOT Be Used to Change Meaning

Keep in mind that the correct usage of ellipses involves leaving out unimportant or unnecessary text, not intentionally changing the meaning or message of the original quotation. Consider the passage below.

Jan Winman's version of *Guys and Dolls* was less than marvelous. It opened Friday night at the Pickwick Playhouse to a packed house. Usually a cheery, fun show, this production was dull. Instead of two hours of smiles and laughs, the audience was bored and fidgety. . .

Here are some correct and incorrect uses of ellipses.

"Jan Winman's version of *Guys and Dolls* . . . opened Friday night." *correct*

"This production was dull . . . the audience was bored and fidgety." *correct*

"Jan Winman's version of *Guys and Dolls* was . . . marvelous." *incorrect*

"A cheery, fun show . . . two hours of smiles . . ." *incorrect*

HYPHENS

When to Use Hyphens

Hyphens are used to join words together.

Use a hyphen to form adjectives with *well* when the adjective comes in front of the noun it is describing (but often not when it comes after).

> **The well-deserved honor was bestowed upon Mrs. Pritchard.**
>
> **It was well deserved.**
>
> **The Gateway Arch is a well-known monument.**
>
> **That monument is well known.**

Hyphens are used to attach other adverbs that do not end in *-ly* to the past-tense form of verbs. Some common adverbs that do not end in *-ly* are *best, most, worst,* and *much.* These word pairs need a hyphen only when they occur before the noun they modify.

> **The best-known character in the book dies at the end.**
>
> **Much-loved comedian Jerry Seinfeld is one of the voices in *Bee Movie* (2007).**

Use a hyphen to connect parts of some compound words. For more on compound words, see page 130.

city-state	merry-go-round	nine-year-old
father-in-law	modern-day	self-defense
great-grandfather	mother-in-law	tongue-tied
grown-up	mother-of-pearl	X-ray

Hyphens are used to make some color words.

> **pinkish-purple**
>
> **reddish-orange**

Use a hyphen with *-elect.*

> **mayor-elect**
>
> **president-elect**

> **LOOK OUT!**
> Do not use a hyphen when the first part of the adverb ends in -ly, or when the compound adjective comes after the noun it describes.

> We use these terms when someone has already won an election but has not yet taken office.

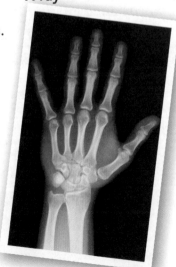

Use hyphens with some last names.

Daniel Day-Lewis

Joseph Gordon-Levitt

Many long words with the prefix *self-* are hyphenated.

self-conscious

self-restraint

Use a hyphen to show a range.

For more on electrons, see pages 18-21.

Grover Cleveland held two nonconsecutive terms as President: 1885-89 and 1893-97.

LOOK OUT!

Do not use a hyphen with some prefixes, such as step- and un-.

- stepbrother
- stepmother
- unlock
- unnecessary

Sometimes, hyphens can be used to clear up confusion between two words. For example, *re-create* (to create again) needs a hyphen so it is not confused with the word *recreate* (to relax and have fun, or to participate in recreation). Here are some more examples of ways hyphens can make clear the meanings of words that might otherwise be misread.

Patty Lou went to the coop to check on the chickens.

Then she went to the co-op to buy some fresh vegetables.

Fred re-covered his sofa after he recovered from the flu.

HYPHENS

Hyphens and Numbers

Use hyphens when writing out compound numbers between 21 and 99.

twenty-six

three hundred fifty-eight

Use hyphens when an age is used as an adjective before a noun.

Patty has a six-year-old brother.

Patty's brother is six years old.

Use a hyphen when a number and a noun work together as an adjective and come before the noun they are describing (but not when they come after).

She ran the 100-meter race.

The race is 100 meters long.

Jim's 524-page book is a best seller.

Jim's best-selling book is 524 pages long.

Use a hyphen when spelling out fractions.

one-half cup

two-thirds majority

Use a hyphen when an ordinal number (such as first or second) and a noun work together as an adjective before a noun.

The Greens live in one of the fourth-floor apartments.

The Greens live in an apartment on the fourth floor.

YOUR TURN!

Hyphen Check

Put a ✓ by the sentences that use hyphens correctly, and draw an ✗ by the ones that use hyphens incorrectly. If any hyphens are missing, write them in.

- Mom, when we go to the park, can I ride the merry go-round?

- My step-brother practices karate.

- I used wood and paint to recreate the sign that was knocked down.

- For the school dance, I have chosen a purplish blue tie.

- Kim is a well-read nine-year-old girl.

- The homework assignment on Marie Curie (1867-1934) is on pages 62-68.

Hyphens at the End of Lines

Hyphens are used to split words when there is not enough room for the entire word to fit on the same line. In general, it is important to break a word at the end of a syllable. Never split a word with only one syllable. Also, avoid leaving one letter alone on a line.

elem- entary	elemen- tary	inter- action

Break words after prefixes and before suffixes, or between double consonants.

pre- historic	renew- able	chan- nel

The hyphen should always appear at the end of the line.

hap- pen *correct*	hap -ppen *incorrect*

LOOK OUT!

Avoid breaking proper nouns (see page 8). Also avoid breaking words in the middle of a blended sound, like *th* or *sh*.

au-   out-
thor   house

In *author*, the *t* and *h* are pronounced together in a single sound, so they should not be broken up. In *outhouse*, the *t* and *h* are pronounced separately.

YOUR TURN!

Curious About Hyphens?

Read the paragraph below about the Mars Science Laboratory, and circle all the hyphens that are used incorrectly.

There is no dream too big for NASA's Jet Propuls-ion Laboratory (JPL). Since it was formed in 1936, JPL has pushed the limits of exploration. By focu-sing primarily on the making of robotic space-craft, this team has repeatedly made histor-y. Currently, the Mars Science Laboratory is one of JPL's largest missions. For decades, the team has been sending instruments, de-vices, and robots to the Red Planet to deter-mine if there has ever been life on Mars. In No--vember 2011, JPL sent a high-tech rover called Curiosity to Mars. The journey was 285 million mil-es (459 million km) long and took eight months.

DASHES

When to Use Dashes

Commas, parentheses (see page 100), and dashes have something in common. All three can be used to set off words or whole sentences that show a break in thought.

The three sentences below are all correct, but their meanings are slightly different.

Henrietta's dog, a purebred Pekingese, won the dog show.

Henrietta's dog (a purebred Pekingese) won the dog show.

Henrietta's dog—a purebred Pekingese—won the dog show.

Similar to the way words, such as *bad, horrible,* and *disastrous,* can have different shades of meaning, using these three punctuation styles can tell you just how important it is that Henrietta's dog is a purebred Pekingese. Here's how.

Commas are the most neutral. ▶ The dog is a Pekingese.

Parentheses indicate that it is not important that the dog is a Pekingese. ▶ You probably don't need to know the dog is a Pekingese, but just in case you were wondering, I thought I'd mention it in passing.

Dashes are the exclamation points of this kind of punctuation. Use them when you want to emphasize something. ▶ That dog is a purebred Pekingese!

Use a dash to show that a speaker has been interrupted (usually in dialogue inside quotation marks, just before the closing quotation mark).

"I can't see a—" she said as she fell into the hole.

Making a Dash

A dash is double the size of a hyphen. Type two hyphens in a row (without a space between them) to make one dash, or use the keystroke for an em-dash.

-- ▶ —

Make Your Mark!

Write the names of each of the punctuation marks
in the Word List in the empty fill-it-in puzzle below.

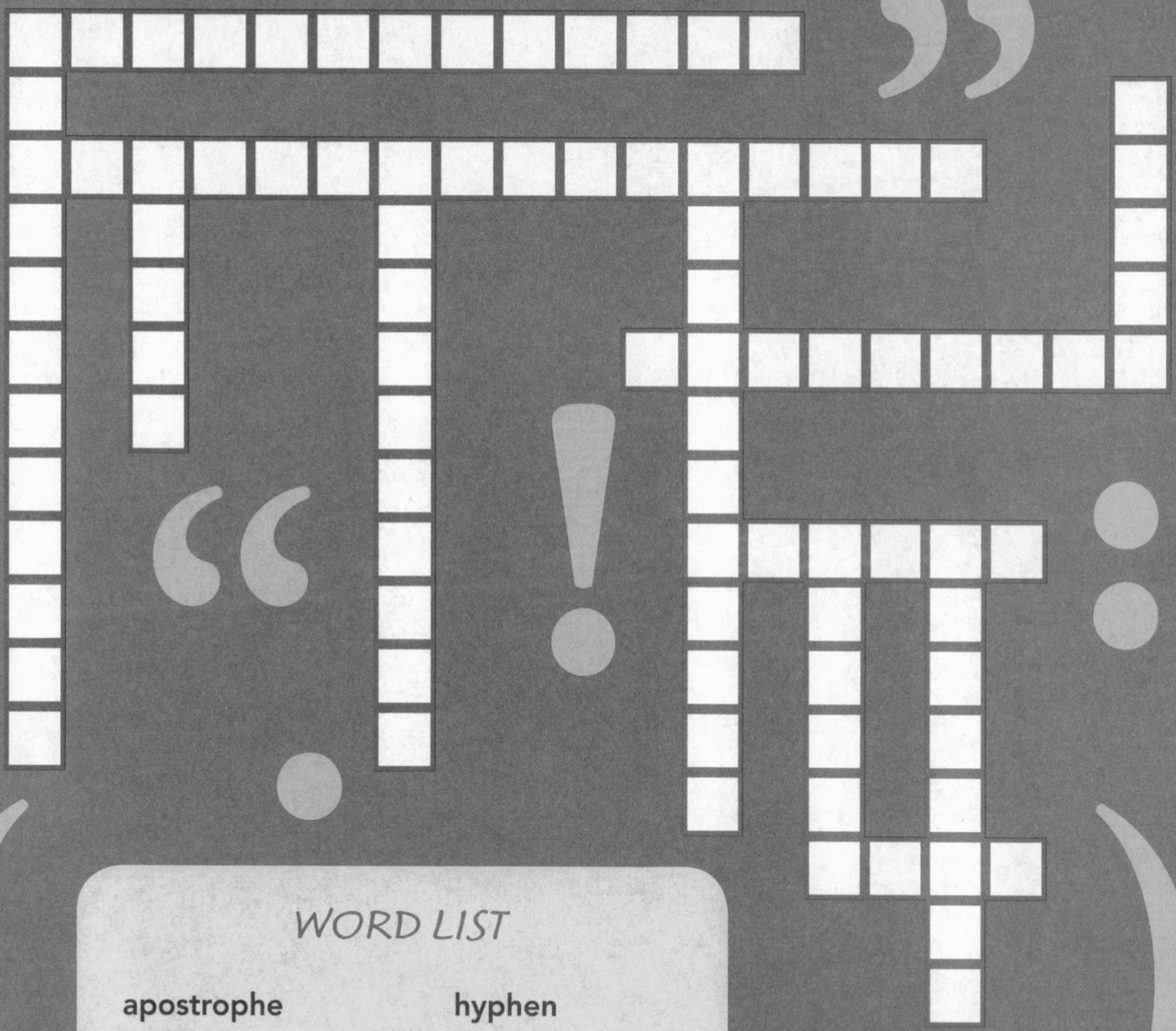

WORD LIST

apostrophe

colon

comma

dash

ellipsis

exclamation point

hyphen

parenthesis

period

question mark

quotation mark

semicolon

USE THE CORRECT WORD EVERY TIME

Your writing can be only as good as the words you use, and choosing the right words can be a challenge. This section will help you choose the right words and spell them correctly every time.

SOUNDALIKES

Words That Sound Like Another Word

It is easy to confuse words that sound exactly alike, even though they are spelled differently and have different meanings. Here are some soundalikes that you are probably familiar with. If there are words on this list that you do not know, take a minute to look them up!

I don't feel well. I ate eight donuts.

Words That Sound Alike			
be	bee	one	won
bear	bare	pair	pear
blew	blue	passed	past
board	bored	peace	piece
break	brake	prince	prints
by	buy, bye	role	roll
close	clothes	rose	rows
days	daze	scene	seen
dear	deer	seam	seem
eight	ate	see	sea
eye	I	steal	steel
find	fined	sun	son
flew	flu	tail	tale
great	grate	to	too, two
hear	here	wait	weight
hole	whole	waste	waist
hour	our	weather	whether
know	no	week	weak
lie	lye	which	witch
made	maid	whirled	world
male	mail	would	wood
meet	meat	write	right

Which One Won?

Fill in the blanks in each sentence with a pair of soundalikes from the chart on page 118. Be sure you write the right word in each spot!

- They spent the _____ day filling in that _____ in the ground.

- The soccer team _____ only _____ game this year.

- Carlos had the flu and felt _____ all _____.

- Rita hated to _____ food, but she wanted a smaller _____.

- The butchers agreed to _____ at the _____ market.

- Wendy went to the beach to _____ the _____.

- The person who delivers our _____ is _____.

- The greedy boy _____ _____ slices of cake.

- There is a _____ about a fox who loses his _____.

- Sarah caught the _____ after she _____ in an airplane.

- Ouch, _____ got something in my _____.

- We were _____, so we played a _____ game.

- Gina did not mean to _____ the _____ on her bicycle.

- It's so noisy, I can't _____ you in _____.

- Zack _____ up a _____ balloon for the birthday party.

- A _____ friend went _____ hunting.

- _____ _____ cast the spell?

- The _____ _____ the bed.

SOUNDALIKES

Other Common Soundalikes

You know the difference between the verb *to be* and the busy, buzzing insect called a bee. But do you know the difference that one letter makes in the words *lightning* and *lightening?* Here are some soundalike pairs, along with their definitions.

Word	Meaning
Capitol	the building that houses the U.S. Congress
capital	an important city
chili	a hot pepper
chilly	cold
complements	goes well with, or completes
compliments	flatters, praises
lightning	a burst of electricity in the sky
lightening	becoming lighter in color, the opposite of darkening
principal	a person in charge
principle	an important idea
stationary	not moving
stationery	writing paper
suite	connected rooms
sweet	having a sugary taste

Possessive Pronouns and Contractions That Sound Alike

Some possessive pronouns sound exactly like some contractions. This chart can help you keep them straight.

Possessive Pronoun	Contraction (Its Meaning)
its	it's (it is)
their	they're (they are)
theirs	there's (there is)
whose	who's (who is)
your	you're (you are)

LOOK OUT!

Their and *they're* both sound just like *there,* too. Pay close attention to make sure you include the right one in your writing.

Show Off Your Skills!

Fill in the blank with the right word. Look at the possessive pronoun and contraction chart on page 120 if you need a hint. Use each word only once.

- I don't know _____ at the door.

- The dog slipped out of _____ collar.

- Phil, is it okay if I give Gail _____ e-mail address?

- I know _____ Saturday, but I still have to go to work.

- I know _____ your grandparents, but they seem too young.

- I can wait till _____ done eating breakfast.

- The twins left _____ bathing suits at the pool.

- Do you know _____ phone this is?

- _____ a spot on my new dress.

- I took mine, not _____.

- Please sit over _____.

121

SOUNDALIKES

Words with Multiple Meanings

A **multiple-meaning word** is a word that has more than one meaning. Though the word's definition, part of speech, and pronunciation may change according to how it is used in a sentence, the spelling of the word stays the same.

Word	Definition #1	Definition #2
hard	the opposite of *soft*	difficult
train	a locomotive or subway	to exercise to prepare for a sporting event
stick	to stay put	a long, thin piece of wood
foot	a body part below the ankle	a measurement equal to 12 inches
punch	a fruity drink	to hit with your fist
rose	a flower	past tense of the verb *to rise*, meaning to get up

YOUR TURN!

Riddle Me This

You know lots of multiple-meaning words that are not in the chart above. Answer each of these riddles with a multiple-meaning word.

You might find this in a cave or next to home plate. What is it?

_____

What can you find at the end of your finger or inside a toolbox?

_____

A dog and a tree both have this. What is it?

_____

It may be a king or a measuring tool. What is it?

_____

What's a Homonym?

You may come across these terms for words that have different meanings but either sound alike or are spelled the same way.

Homonyms are words with the same spelling or sound but different meanings.

Homophones are words that sound alike but are spelled differently, like *write* and *right*. The chart on page 118 includes many examples of homophones.

Homographs are words that are spelled the same but have different meanings, like *right* (direction) and *right* (correct). The **multiple-meaning** words on page 122 are homographs.

A **heteronym** is a type of homograph. In this case, two words have the same spelling but are pronounced differently.

minute (tiny)

This word sounds like my-NEWT.

minute (measurement of time)

This word sounds like MIN-it.

Homonyms, homophones, homographs, and heteronyms all have root words that come from the Greek language.

homo means "same"
phon means "sound"
graph means "write"
hetero means "different"

PICTURE PAIRS

There is one word that can describe each of the pictures in these pairs. Write the multiple-meaning word for each pair on the lines below.

_____

_____

_____

_____

_____

_____

COMMON MISTAKES

Easily Confused Words

The words in this chart are often confused because they look or sound like each other.

Word	Meaning
accept	to take or receive something offered
except	other than
affect	to influence or change
effect	a result or consequence
breath	air breathed in or out
breathe	to inhale and exhale
calendar	a chart that shows the days and months of the year
colander	a kitchen strainer
desert	a dry region
dessert	a sweet end to a meal
immigrate	to move to a new country
emigrate	to leave a country to live somewhere else
lay	to place something down on something else
lie	to recline, as in bed (or say something untrue)
loose	not tight
lose	not win, misplace
pitcher	a container for liquids
picture	an image or a photo
then	next
than	compared to

Dessert in the desert

Quirky Crossword

To complete the crossword puzzle below, fill in the blanks with words from the chart on page 124.

Hint for #15

ACROSS

2. Anastasia posted a _____ of her cat on Facebook.

4. Eating junk food can _____ your health.

8. I _____ my books on the counter every day when I get home from school.

9. Many people _____ to the United States from other countries hoping for a better life.

10. Everyone, _____ Greg, passed the test.

11. The chemistry experiment showed the _____ of gravity on falling objects.

12. Ice cream is Miriam's favorite _____.

13. The rain came first, _____ thunder.

14. Did you _____ your mittens again?

15. Sam can hold his _____ for two minutes.

18. Dina's family decided to _____ from Greece.

19. I _____ this award on behalf of my husband, who could not be with us tonight.

DOWN

1. Carla trained her dog to _____ down on the mat.

3. Some dogs are smarter _____ others.

5. Pico checked the school _____ to see which week was spring break.

6. Jules had a stuffy nose and had to _____ through his mouth.

7. Mom put a _____ of lemonade on the table.

14. Anna's little brother has a _____ tooth.

16. Josh used a _____ to strain the cooked spaghetti.

17. The middle of Australia is mostly _____.

125

COMMON MISTAKES

Good vs. Well

Many people confuse *good* and *well*.

Good is an adjective. It is used to describe nouns.

> **That was a good movie.**
>
> **It's hard to find good tomatoes this time of year.**

Well is an adverb. It tells "how."

> **Jane sings well.**
>
> **Jon writes well.**

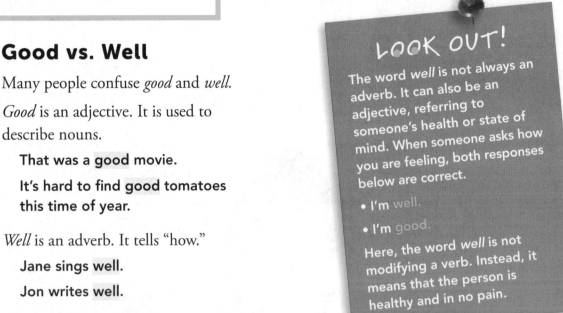

LOOK OUT!

The word *well* is not always an adverb. It can also be an adjective, referring to someone's health or state of mind. When someone asks how you are feeling, both responses below are correct.

- I'm well.
- I'm good.

Here, the word *well* is not modifying a verb. Instead, it means that the person is healthy and in no pain.

Here's an example of a common mistake involving the word *good*.

> **The basketball team played good last night.** *incorrect*

The sentence above is wrong. The writer is explaining how the team played. *To play* is a verb, so the writer should use an adverb, not an adjective, to describe how the teamed played.

> ── *adverb*
>
> **The basketball team played (well) last night.** *correct*

Both *good* and *well* have the same comparative and superlative:

> **ADJECTIVE: good ⧐ better ⧐ best**
>
> **ADVERB: well ⧐ better ⧐ best**

Bad vs. Badly

Just like *good* and *well*, *bad* and *badly* have the same comparative and superlative:

ADJECTIVE: bad ▶ worse ▶ worst

ADVERB: badly ▶ worse ▶ worst

Many people—including adults—confuse when they should use the words *bad* and *badly*. They use an adjective when they should use an adverb.

The losing team played bad. *incorrect*   *adjective*

Here you can see *bad* and *badly* used correctly:

The crowd booed when the umpire made a bad call. *correct*

The losing team played badly. *correct*

adverb

B O O O O O o o !

YOUR TURN!

Show How Well You Know the Difference

Fill in the blanks with the right choice of words.

• Jess doesn't speak Spanish very _____.
(good/well)

• Walt had a _____ time at the beach.
(good/well)

• It's _____ to be here with you all for Thanksgiving.
(good/well)

• I wanted that cookie so _____.
(bad/badly)

• His new business did _____ its first year.
(good/well)

• Too much sugar is _____ for you.
(bad/badly)

COMMON MISTAKES

Common Word Misunderstandings

Some vocabulary mistakes occur so often you might not even notice them.

Itch vs. scratch

An itch is a feeling, not an action. Pulling your nails across your skin is scratching, not itching.

> **SIMON:** My arm itches so much. This poison ivy is driving me nuts.

> **SIMON'S MOM:** Don't scratch it! You'll get a scar.

Fewer vs. less

If you can count it, use *fewer*. If you can't, use *less*.

> **We have fewer envelopes now than when we started sending out thank-you cards.**

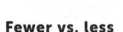

> **The school is less effective with fewer teachers.**

A school can be more or less effective, but you can't count effectiveness the way you can count the number of teachers.

Farther vs. further

Use *farther* when you are talking about a physical distance that could be measured. If you are not talking about things that are a real distance apart, use *further*.

> **Grandma Dora lives farther away than Grandma Priscilla.**

> **The pool will be closed until further notice.**

May I Come In?

Many people stumble over the difference between *can* and *may*. The word *can* means "be able to" or "be capable of," and *may* is used to ask permission.

Four-year-old Will can tie his shoes by himself.

May I please be excused?

Suppose you need to use the restroom at school. You know how to use the restroom, so there is no doubt you can go to the restroom. However, you still need to ask permission: May I go to the restroom?

Don't Always Sound It Out

When you were little, you may have learned to read by sounding words out. However, sometimes spelling words the way they sound can get you into trouble, especially with contractions that end with **'ve.**

I should have known that! *correct*

I should of known that! *incorrect*

The contraction *should've* sounds like *should of*— but don't spell it that way!

That's Not Even a Word!

Some people use words that aren't words at all. Don't get caught using these misspellings of common words.

INCORRECT	CORRECT
alot	a lot
noone	no one
anyways	anyway

YOUR TURN!

What's the Right Word?

Fill in the blanks with the correct word choice.

• I did not know you were in town, or I would _____ invited
  (of/have)
  you to my party.

• Rebecca has eaten _____ calories since she began her new diet.
  (fewer/less)

• Jack felt _____ self-conscious after he got his braces off.
  (fewer/less)

• The weather did not _____ my decision
  (affect/effect)
  to stay home on Saturday.

• When my dog curls up near my feet, I can feel its
  _____ on my ankles.
  (breath/breathe)

• Paula _____ her chin whenever she
  (itched/scratched)
  was concentrating on a problem.

• The mosquito bite on her leg _____.
  (itched/scratched)

COMMON MISTAKES

Compound Words

A **compound** word is two or more words used together.

You use compound words all the time. Compound words can be tricky to spell correctly because some are one word and others are two words. Some even take a hyphen.

An **open compound word** has a space between the words.

> air conditioner
> board game
> first aid
> full moon
> half sister
> high school
> ice cream
> lawn mower
> post office

Hyphenated compound words are kept together with a hyphen or hyphens.

> city-state
> first-rate
> grown-up
> merry-go-round
> mother-in-law
> self-defense
> T-shirt
> water-repellent
> well-being

Closed compound words do not have a space between them. Here's a handy list of many closed compounds. Look over the list. Did you know that each of these terms is spelled as one word?

> applesauce
> backache
> blackboard
> campfire
> cheerleader
> cupcake
> doorknob
> driveway
> earthquake
> earthworm
> eyeball
> fingernail
> football
> girlfriend
> homemade
> jellyfish
> lifeguard
> lightbulb

> lipstick
> litterbug
> motorcycle
> newspaper
> notebook
> oatmeal
> peanut
> ponytail
> raincoat
> shipwreck
> snowman
> sunflower
> toothbrush
> underground
> watermelon
> waterproof
> wheelchair
> windmill

LOOK OUT!

Compound adjectives often use hyphens, but only when they come *before* a noun.

- I have a part-time job.
- I work part time.

For more about hyphens, see pages 110–113.

One Word or Two?

Sometimes a compound word has a meaning that is different from that of the two words written separately. For example, *everyday* means "ordinary" or "used routinely." Everyday clothes are different from the fancy suits or dresses a person might wear to a wedding.

Do you brush your teeth every day? *correct*

Do you brush your teeth everyday? *incorrect*

For many children, chores are part of everyday life. *correct*

For many children, chores are part of every day life. *incorrect*

Many children do chores every day. *correct*

Here are some other examples.

Already means "before now" or "so soon." *All ready* means "completely prepared" or that each member in a group is prepared.

I already saw this movie.

She was all ready to go scuba diving.

They were all ready to start the road trip.

Sometime means "at an unspecified time in the future." *Some time* refers to a period of time.

Stop by sometime.

I'm going to spend some time going through my sock drawer and throwing away the ones with holes.

Anyone is a pronoun that does not refer to a specific person. It refers to any person. *Any one* refers to a specific, but unidentified, person or thing.

Does anyone know the time?

If any one of my 20 goldfish died, I would be devastated.

Compounds Can Be Formed over Time

It takes time for people to get used to new compound words. A compound word, such as *health care,* starts out as two words. In time, it may end up in the dictionary as *healthcare.* Right now, you may notice that different newspapers and magazines spell it differently.

health care ▸ health-care? ▸ healthcare?

YOUR TURN!

Test Your Knowledge

Draw a ✓ next to the sentences that use the right word. Put an ✗ next to the ones that don't.

- Who cares, any way?

- The twins are all ready to go.

- Every one is invited to my party.

- I maybe able to come to your party.

- Nancy all ways wears her hair in a ponytail.

- I can't find any body who took notes during that class.

- My mother usually answers maybe when I ask her a question.

- I will solve this problem any way I can!

- Aidan all ready has a date for the prom.

SPELLING

Common Word Endings

A **suffix** is a common word ending that changes the meaning of a root word. Here are a few spelling rules to help you add suffixes correctly.

Drop the final **-e** in a word when adding a suffix that begins with a vowel. If the suffix begins with a consonant, keep the final **-e.**

hope ▶ hoping ▶ hopeful

care ▶ caring ▶ careful

move ▶ moving ▶ movement

What if a word ends in **-y?** Change the final **y** to an **i,** if the final **y** follows a consonant.

happy ▶
happiness
pity ▶ pitiful

LOOK OUT!

When adding a suffix that begins with a vowel to a word that ends in -y, don't change the final y to an i.

try ▶ trying
buy ▶ buying

YOUR TURN!

Building Blocks

Look for words you know that include the root words on the left and the suffixes on the right. Draw lines from root words to suffixes, and write each new word on the lines below. You may use root words and suffixes as many times as you want to make as many new words as possible.

ROOT WORDS +	SUFFIXES =		
act	-or	_____	_____
edit	-er	_____	_____
paint	-ful	_____	_____
dance	-age	_____	_____
block	-like	_____	_____
pilgrim	-ment	_____	_____
life	-ship	_____	_____
child	-ish	_____	_____
govern	-less	_____	_____
friend		_____	_____
self		_____	_____
hope		_____	_____
joy		_____	_____
care		_____	_____

Frequently Misspelled Word Endings

Here are some groups of words with endings that sound the same but are spelled differently.

Words That End with -ent and -ant

consistent	ignorant
frequent	instant
resident	servant

Words That End with -tion and -sion

ambition	decision
humiliation	division
occupation	permission
transportation	session

Words That End with -ence and -ance

independence	annoyance
existence	maintenance
occurrence	resistance

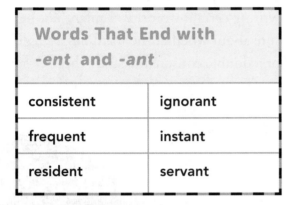

Words That End with -ible and -able

collectible	acceptable
flexible	capable
gullible	changeable
horrible	comfortable
legible	durable
possible	learnable
sensible	notable
terrible	walkable

PLAY THE ODDS

The suffix -able is much more common than -ible. Many words have been (and will be) made by adding the suffix -able to indicate that something is doable.

- "Is it possible to break that vase?" "Yes, the vase is breakable."

- "Can I walk to the museum, or will I need a ride?" "It's walkable."

SPELLING

Spelling Secrets

Here are some common spelling mistakes, as well as some helpful spelling rules (and exceptions).

Words with the **vowel combinations** *ie* and *ei* are often misspelled. Here are some words to remember.

Words with *ei*	Words with *ie*
weird	friend
receive	believe
neighbor	science
weigh	piece
height	ancient
foreign	chief

C's that sound like *s*'s can trip up some spellers. Both *sit* and *city* begin with the same *s* sound. Here are more words with *c*'s that sound like *s*'s.

- civil
- century
- celebrate
- cyclist

Sometimes, a *c* in the middle of a word can also sound like an *s*.

- receive
- license
- recipe

Double consonants are often the cause of spelling confusion. When you are writing certain words, you might not be sure about whether the word has a single or a double consonant. Study these words, and try to remember which consonants appear twice.

- accident
- across
- address
- apartment
- broccoli
- canister
- committee
- disappear
- disappoint
- embarrass
- finally
- interrupt
- necessary
- occasion
- omit
- pavilion
- recommend
- tomorrow

The letters *f, l,* and *s* are often doubled at the end of a word.

- ball
- cliff
- drill
- miss
- pass
- staff

When to Double a Consonant

Sometimes you need to double a final consonant when you add a suffix, or word ending. This is often the case for words that end in a single consonant (other than *c* and *x*).

ban ▸ banned

get ▸ getting

slip ▸ slipped

LOOK OUT!

There are exceptions to the consonant-doubling rule. If a word ends in *c*, add a *k* before the suffix.

panic ▸ panicky

picnic ▸ picnicking

Do not double the *x*:

box ▸ boxed

wax ▸ waxing

YOUR TURN!

Double Up!

Each of these words has an antonym (a word with the opposite meaning) that ends with a double consonant. Write the antonym after each word.

- flexible _____*stiff*_____

- short _____

- prince _____

- on _____

- empty _____

- none _____

- more _____

- push _____

- buy _____

- sharp, exciting _____

Commonly Misspelled Words

Here are 60 words that are often spelled incorrectly. Look over the list. Which ones give you the most trouble? If there are any words on this list that you are not familiar with, look them up in the dictionary.

acceptable

accidentally

accommodate

ache

apparent

argument

barbecue

believe

buoy

business

calendar

category

ceiling

cemetery

changeable

collectible

definitely

discipline

dumbbell

embarrass

environment

equipment

equipped

exercise

experience

explanation

fascinating

grateful

guarantee

hierarchy

immediate

intelligence

interruption

judgment

ketchup

khaki

library

license

maneuver

marriage

medieval

miniature

misspell

mysterious

occasionally

pastime

phlegm

playwright

psychology

restaurant

rhyme

rhythm

schedule

scissors

sergeant

strength

temperature

twelfth

until

vacuum

Giant Word Search

Find all **60** words listed on page 136 in the grid below. They appear forward, backward, up, down, and diagonally. Circle each one.

S	E	R	G	E	A	N	T	D	E	P	P	I	U	Q	E	T	N	E	M	U	G	R	A	G
R	F	T	H	G	I	R	W	Y	A	L	P	W	D	M	I	N	I	A	T	U	R	E	B	N
O	S	O	X	A	K	P	E	P	D	E	U	E	X	P	L	A	N	A	T	I	O	N	E	I
S	U	T	C	Z	P	H	L	E	W	G	H	D	M	L	T	R	E	M	I	D	F	O	X	T
S	E	T	R	C	O	W	F	H	G	P	C	B	E	O	G	U	A	R	A	N	T	E	E	A
I	C	J	U	E	A	I	T	T	I	D	T	U	E	H	C	A	K	E	B	I	N	B	R	N
C	N	H	R	H	N	S	H	E	P	T	E	X	P	T	C	T	F	O	Y	E	P	P	C	I
S	E	T	F	I	P	G	I	K	A	H	K	E	N	E	W	S	P	D	X	G	J	Y	I	C
B	G	N	T	E	L	Z	T	O	D	L	I	G	M	D	X	E	M	B	A	R	R	A	S	S
R	I	E	Y	R	I	O	E	H	N	N	J	E	T	N	E	R	A	P	P	A	J	O	E	A
A	L	M	L	A	I	E	L	P	B	A	T	K	X	U	C	M	R	N	R	T	R	U	Q	F
Y	L	N	L	R	R	R	B	M	A	E	L	I	Y	B	H	Q	J	B	H	E	E	K	U	E
G	E	O	A	C	E	U	I	Z	R	I	M	L	I	T	N	U	I	P	X	F	L	A	I	S
O	T	R	T	H	V	T	T	Y	B	B	Z	A	Y	K	D	L	X	H	M	U	B	M	P	N
L	N	I	N	Y	U	A	C	L	E	Q	D	H	O	G	T	O	M	W	I	L	A	E	M	E
O	I	V	E	V	E	R	E	O	C	G	R	I	M	M	E	D	I	A	T	E	E	C	E	C
H	U	N	D	I	N	E	L	G	U	I	Z	E	V	J	C	E	I	L	I	N	G	N	N	I
C	P	E	I	Q	A	P	L	N	E	E	N	I	L	P	I	C	S	I	D	J	N	E	T	L
Y	A	C	C	O	M	M	O	D	A	T	E	E	L	B	A	T	P	E	C	C	A	I	M	L
S	S	V	C	N	H	E	C	Z	J	L	Y	B	E	L	I	E	V	E	M	Y	H	R	J	E
P	T	O	A	A	V	T	A	M	R	O	D	U	M	B	B	E	L	L	U	C	C	E	F	P
N	I	A	G	C	A	L	E	N	D	A	R	O	S	S	E	N	I	S	U	B	U	P	T	S
J	M	G	E	L	H	P	R	F	M	Y	M	Y	R	O	G	E	T	A	C	O	D	X	O	S
U	E	G	A	I	R	R	A	M	Y	S	T	E	R	I	O	U	S	M	A	N	T	E	F	I
I	N	T	E	R	R	U	P	T	I	O	N	J	D	U	N	K	L	A	V	E	I	D	E	M

SLANG

Avoid Informal Language

Sometimes you lounge around the house in an old, ripped shirt and sweats. Sometimes you get dressed up to go out for a special occasion. Language is like this too. **Informal language** is relaxed. You can break the rules and show your personality. **Formal language** is more structured; grammar and spelling count! You use formal English when you write a report for school or give a speech.

2 txt or Not 2 txt?

You write more informally when you leave a note for your parents than when you compose an essay for school. But some kids write messages with abbreviations (like "U" for "you"), no capitalization ("i saw leslie"), and phonetic spellings ("sez" for "says"). Using texting language like "lol" or "cuz" (for because) or "☺" in their school writing, rather than saving it for texting friends, is a mistake.

Text messaging can be an effective way to communicate, but you need to know when to use texting abbreviations and when to avoid them. Do not use texting language in schoolwork, on tests, or when writing Grandma a thank-you note. It's easy to figure out what kind of language to use. You do it all the time when you speak. Think about your audience before you write, and decide whether it is okay to use informal language. Then, have fun!

LOOK OUT!

Many students assume that the language often used in texting originated with cell phones. Actually, most of these shortcuts have been around for decades. Some abbreviations, like "b/c" for "because" or "btw" for "by the way," were used long before computers.

YOUR TURN!

What Do You Think?

Some people think text messaging is wonderful. However, others worry that texting language is harming written English. What do you think? Does text messaging lead to the acceptance of bad grammar and poor spelling? Write an answer to this question that gives your opinions in your own words. Use formal language.

_____

_____

_____

_____

_____

What Is Slang?

Slang is informal language used by a particular group at a certain time. "Groovy" and "hip" were once popular slang words. If you say "That's hot!"—and you're not talking about something just out of the oven—you're using slang too. Kids today may not know the slang their parents used when they were young, and today's slang will sound old-fashioned in the future.

People don't always understand another group's slang. That's why you shouldn't use it when you are writing for adults who are not your parents or close friends. Other adults who don't know you may not understand what you are trying to say. They may even think you are being disrespectful. So save slang for your friends.

Far out!

Can you dig it?

Is It Slang?

Some slang is so common you may not even realize the word is slang. When you use these words to mean something different from their dictionary definitions, you're using slang.

whatever	gonna	hot
no worries	dunno	sez
awesome	geek	lol

KEEP IT CLEAN!
Dirty words and curse words have no place in formal writing or casual notes (and you should try to avoid them altogether).

READY TO WRITE

Writing is a way to share useful information. It's also a way to communicate your thoughts and feelings. Do you want to know the secret to becoming a better writer? Write, write, and write some more! Begin a journal. Write long letters to friends and family members. Take a lot of notes during class. Start a blog.

FICTION AND NONFICTION

Tips for Writing Fiction

- Use your imagination.
- Tell the story in order.
- Draw pictures.

Types of Writing

There are many different kinds of writing. The **two biggest categories** of literature are fiction, which features imaginary characters and stories, and nonfiction, which includes facts and is about real people, places, and events. Writing can be grouped into categories called genres. A genre (*zhan*-rah) can be a general category, like fiction. Or it can be more specific, like science fiction or historical fiction.

What Is Fiction?

Fiction is as rich and varied as your own imagination. It includes folktales, fairy tales, fables, mysteries, and stories about people like you.

Fantasy stories often have magical characters. They often take place in magical places where anything can happen. *Alice in Wonderland* is a fantasy story.

Fables are stories that teach a lesson or moral. They may have animal characters. *The Tortoise and the Hare* is a fable. So is *The Grasshopper and the Ant.*

Folktales and **fairy tales** usually contain pretend characters such as elves or animals that can talk. Folk and fairy tales may begin "Once upon a time." *Stone Soup* is a folktale. *Hansel and Gretel* is a fairy tale.

Historical fiction stories or novels take place during a particular historical period. The people, events, and settings from the past may be real, but the story comes from the writer's imagination.

Mystery stories usually tell about a crime that is being solved.

Romance stories have love as a central theme.

Science fiction stories generally take place in the future or in a setting where scientific discoveries and advanced technology play important parts in the plot.

What Is Nonfiction?

Nonfiction is a kind of writing that includes true stories about you, or personal narratives. It also includes true stories about other people, or biographies, and histories, which describe events and places in the past. News stories, reports, and reviews are also nonfiction.

A **personal narrative,** or autobiography, tells a story about something that happened to you.

A **report** gives facts about a topic. Writers find facts in different books, magazines, and resources. Writers may also include charts, graphs, maps, diagrams, and photographs to help readers better understand their report.

A **news story** gives important facts about a person, place, object, event, or idea. A news story has a headline that tells what the story is about. News stories often explain something or provide readers with new information.

Tips for Writing Nonfiction

- Write about real people, real animals, and real events.

- Check your facts.

- Use photographs, charts, illustrations, and other graphic items.

Tools for a Writer

Reference books contain nonfiction writing. Here are some examples of reference books that you might consult while writing.

A **THESAURUS** is filled with synonyms, which are words with similar meanings, and antonyms, which are words that have opposite meanings.

A **DICTIONARY** contains words' spellings, pronunciations, origins, meanings, and examples of usage.

ENCYCLOPEDIAS have lots of entries explaining and describing various topics.

ALMANACS offer readers quick-and-easy access to facts, figures, charts, and other data for a specific year.

An **ATLAS** contains maps. The maps might show the political makeup of a region, display the elevation and surface features of an area, or contain historical information.

THE WRITING PROCESS

Write in Stages

Think of writing as a process, a series of **steps** that can help you become a better writer.

PREWRITE

First, plan what you will write.

- What will I write about?
- What will I say?
- How will I organize it?
- Who is my audience? (Who will read it?)
- What is the purpose of my writing?

DRAFT

You'll do most of your writing in this step. Use your notes from your prewriting activities to get all your ideas down on paper. Don't worry about mistakes. You can fix those later.

- What ideas do I want to include?
- How can I organize my ideas?
- How do I get my ideas on paper?

Get Inspired!

Start your own personal **writer's notebook**. Keep it with you so you can write anywhere and anytime. Then be aware. Make notes in your notebook about things you see and hear.

- Set aside a few minutes before you go to bed to write about your day. Did anything strange happen at school? Did someone tell you a funny joke or story? Write it down.

- Next time you go on a trip, bring your writer's notebook. Write descriptions of the new places and things you see.

- Do you have a favorite TV show? Imagine you are in an episode. What happens to you? What do you say? Write all about it in your writer's notebook.

EDIT AND PROOFREAD

It's time to find and fix any mistakes.

> Did I use correct punctuation?

> Are there capital letters in all the right places?

> Did I check my spelling?

> Are all my sentences complete?

REVISE

Go over your first draft, and make it better. Share your writing with other readers to get their suggestions.

> Is my main idea clear?

> Do I have enough details?

> Is it clear how my ideas fit together?

> Are my sentences well written?

> Have I left out anything important?

PUBLISH

You're all done writing! Now it's time to hand in your work or share your writing with others.

> How do I feel about my writing?

> How do I share my writing with others?

> Will adding graphics help make my point?

PREWRITE

Before You Begin Writing

Prewriting is an essential first step in the writing process. First, you need to **choose a topic** to write about. Sometimes a teacher will assign a topic. Sometimes you can choose your own topic. The topic is the main idea you will write about. Different types of writing require different approaches. If you are writing a news or nonfiction piece, for example, you will need to do research and maybe even conduct interviews before you write. If you are writing fiction, you will need to think about your characters and setting.

What's the Big Idea?

- So where do writers get their ideas? **Writers get ideas from the world around them.** They write about people they know, places they see, activities they do, and things that interest them.

- Writers **look and listen.** They notice colors, sounds, and smells. Then they write.

- **Make lists.** Lists, like the ones below, can help you come up with topics to write about. You can keep your lists in your writer's notebook. Then, when you need an idea to write about, you'll already have some written down.

 YOUR TURN!

List Mania

Here are a few ideas for the kinds of lists you might keep in your writer's notebook. Two of them are about you in real life. One of them might just inspire you to write a fiction story.

Amazing Places I Have Visited

_____

_____

_____

_____

 **Weird Animals I Want to Know More About**

_____

_____

_____

Imagine you were in your friend's attic and you stumbled across an old trunk. What are five things that could be inside that trunk that could change your life?

1._____

2._____

3._____

4._____

5._____

Narrow Down Your Topic

Some topics may be too big to write about easily in one piece of writing. **Think about your topic as a question** you plan to answer in your writing. If your question is too broad, narrow it down.

When you narrow down your topic, make sure it is **open-ended.** This means your topic question can be answered in different ways. If you can answer your topic question with a *yes* or a *no* or by just writing a list, it is not open-ended and you should rethink it. Here's an example.

TOPIC: Endangered animals

QUESTION: Which animals are endangered?   *This question is not open-ended. It could be answered by a long list.*

BETTER QUESTION: Why are African elephants endangered?

Come Up with a Cool Question

> Look back at the lists on page 146. Pick four subjects, and write topic questions for each. If your topic question is too broad, narrow it down.

Topic: _____

Question: _____

Better Question: _____

Topic: _____

Question: _____

Better Question: _____

Topic: _____

Question: _____

Better Question: _____

Topic: _____

Question: _____

Better Question: _____

PREWRITE

Get Organized!

After you've narrowed down your topic, it's time to **organize your ideas.** This is when you decide which ideas and information you want to include in your writing and how you might order those ideas.

Jot down your ideas on a piece of paper. Notes and story organizers can help you create a picture of what you will be writing. There are many ways to use story organizers. Choose the one that makes sense for your topic and the kind of writing you are doing.

Learned about Native Americans

Saw cool plants

Rode in a swamp buggy

Visit to the swamp

Ate frogs' legs

Looked for panther tracks

Spotted an alligator

A **writing web** is one type of organizer. Write your topic in the center. Draw arrows from the topic circle to each of your ideas. Include everything you can think of related to your topic. This is a good way to brainstorm your topic and get started.

A **Venn diagram** is helpful when a homework assignment asks you to compare and contrast.

BUTTERFLIES
• Fly around during the daytime
• Have knobs at the end of their antennas
• Rest with their wings standing upright

BOTH
• Are insects
• Have a long tongue called a proboscis
• Drink flower nectar

MOTHS
• Fly around at night
• Have antennas that look like feathers
• Rest with their wings lying flat

To help you see the order of events in your story, try using **sequence charts,** or story maps. How many boxes you use depends on what you are writing. If you are writing a short story, you may need only three boxes to tell what happens at the beginning, in the middle, and at the end. You can use sequence charts with more than three boxes to map out a sequence of events in history, or the steps to follow in a how-to guide.

Fiction Sequence Chart

BEGINNING	While helping elderly Mrs. Coppin clean her house, Maggie finds a magical necklace. She puts it on and is suddenly transported back in time into a traveling circus.
MIDDLE	Maggie learns many things about Mrs. Coppin's life as a young trapeze artist. Maggie also performs a trapeze trick, learns how to juggle, and even pets a lion. She meets the magician who gave the necklace to Mrs. Coppin.
END	Maggie learns the secret of the necklace, takes it off, and reappears at Mrs. Coppin's house just in time to get home for dinner.

Nonfiction Sequence Chart

EVENT #1	Archaeologist Lee Berger and his family traveled to South Africa to participate in an archaeological dig.
EVENT #2	While walking around near his father's dig site, Berger's nine-year-old son, Matthew, stumbled on a fossil.
EVENT #3	Scientists unearthed the fossil and a few more nearby.
EVENT #4	The fossilized bones turned out to belong to a child who lived two million years ago.
EVENT #5	Researchers studied the fossils and determined that this human ancestor had hips and legs like a modern human but arms like an ape. Scientists now know much more about this species than they knew before.

Make Your Own Map Look back at the lists you wrote on page 146, and choose a story to map out. Draw and fill in a story organizer to help you collect your thoughts.

PREWRITE

Do Some Research

Sometimes you will need to do research to gather more information to write a news article or answer topic questions. Look for facts, definitions, details, quotations, and examples that are relevant to your topic. Begin by making a list of questions you have or your readers may have. Then decide what resources you will need to use to answer your questions. Even when writing fiction, you may want to research a real place or historical time period to make your story more believable and interesting.

Choose Your Resources

Your classroom and school library may have nonfiction books about your topic. You can also check encyclopedias. Take clear notes on the information you find. Use index cards or a notepad. If you are typing your notes on a laptop, be sure to save your files with helpful, descriptive names so you can easily find them later. Keep careful notes about the books you use. Look for documentaries and videos that relate to your topic. These can provide important facts and interesting details to include in your writing. Take notes as you watch.

LOOK OUT!

The website Wikipedia is very popular. Many people use it as an online encyclopedia to find out about a topic. Browsing Wikipedia may help you get ideas. However, Wikipedia is not a reliable website for research. The information there may not be correct or current.

Using the Web

The Internet is a good resource for gathering information when you are writing a research paper. Be sure you choose reliable websites. When using a search engine to find online resources, use the *advanced search* function, and limit your search results to websites that end in *.gov* or *.edu*. These types of websites provide the most reliable information. Be sure to list the websites you used for research at the end of any papers you write for school.

LOOK OUT!

Remember to write your ideas in your own words. Presenting someone else's words as your own is called *plagiarism*, and it is wrong. You can use text from another source in your paper so long as you identify its source.

Conduct Interviews

An interview is a question-and-answer session with another person. Interviews are another way writers get the information they need to answer their topic questions. Interviews are also helpful when you write a news article or other nonfiction article in which you need an expert's knowledge and opinions. An interview can take place in person, in writing, over the phone, or by e-mail. When you use quotes from your interviews in your writing, the quotes must have quotation marks around them. You must also give that person's name in your text.

Interviewing Tips

- **Know what you want to ask.** Write down your questions even if you are doing an in-person interview.

- **Send your questions ahead of time.** That way, the person you interview will have time to think about them.

- **Take clear notes** so you remember the answers. Or you can conduct the interview by e-mail.

- **Be polite and friendly,** and remember to say "thank you" at the end of the interview.

 YOUR TURN!

Put On Your Reporter's Cap

Think about all the interesting people in your life, and choose someone you would like to interview. Perhaps it is your parent, grandparent, or other family member. Maybe you'd like to learn more about a teacher, neighbor, or local business owner. What would this person be able to share with you? Does he or she have an interesting hobby or work in a job you find fascinating? Has he or she had a life experience that you'd like to hear about? Now sit down and write 10 questions that you'd like to ask.

1._____

2._____

3._____

4._____

5._____

6._____

7._____

8._____

9._____

10._____

DRAFT

Put Your Ideas on Paper

Now that you have planned what you will write, it's time to get started on your first draft. Use your notes and story organizers to write sentences and paragraphs about your ideas. Each paragraph should focus on one main idea with details, examples, facts, or opinions about that idea.

Don't worry about making mistakes as you write. A first draft is your beginning attempt to write something. It is a chance to get all your ideas down on paper. A first draft is not supposed to be perfect.

Introduce the Topic

A strong beginning should clearly define your topic and capture readers' attention. Depending on the type of writing, you may want to give your opinion about the topic. Starting with a question or a surprise will make your audience want to read more.

WEAK INTRODUCTION	Dinosaurs used to be alive a long time ago.
STRONG INTRODUCTION	Dinosaurs ruled the land during the Jurassic period, which is why scientists call it the Age of Dinosaurs.

Write a Catchy Opening

Take a look at these strong beginnings.

BEGIN WITH A QUESTION.	Why did dinosaurs become extinct at a time when so many other animals survived?
BEGIN WITH A QUOTATION.	"It has been argued that dinosaurs did not die out but just evolved wings and flew away," said scientist Jamilla Sanders.
BEGIN WITH A DESCRIPTION.	The oceans teemed with life during the Jurassic period.

Main Body Paragraphs

Each body paragraph should focus on one main idea (topic sentence) and include supporting details. The story organizer below can help you plan your paragraphs. Order your information logically. You may wish to put your strongest reason last so readers remember it most clearly.

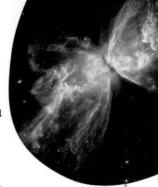

> **MAIN IDEA** The Hubble Space Telescope has taken photographs of many interesting things in space.

> **SUPPORTING DETAIL #1** It has captured one of the clearest pictures ever taken of Jupiter.

> **SUPPORTING DETAIL #2** One photo, taken by Hubble, shows a dying star that looks like a butterfly.

> **SUPPORTING DETAIL #3** Other photos show the colorful clouds of dust that are known as nebulas.

> **SUPPORTING DETAIL #4** Hubble has taken tens of thousands of photos since it was first launched in 1990.

YOUR TURN!

Support Your Argument

Make your own story organizer for an opinion paragraph. Think of a topic that you have a strong opinion about, and write it in the top box. Fill in the other boxes with your supporting arguments. Make sure to include facts and details that support your main idea.

> **MAIN IDEA**

> **SUPPORTING DETAIL #1**

> **SUPPORTING DETAIL #2**

> **SUPPORTING DETAIL #3**

> **SUPPORTING DETAIL #4**

Reach a Conclusion

Finish your draft with a concluding statement. The conclusion at the end of an explanatory piece summarizes the main idea and brings the piece to a logical close. Without a conclusion, a piece of writing does not feel finished. Sometimes a conclusion makes a point as well as summarizes the main idea. The conclusion of an opinion essay often suggests an action that should be taken.

REVISE

Reread and Revise

When you have finished your draft, read it over carefully.
Here are some questions to ask yourself as you read.

Think about the ideas you have covered. Are they clear?

Have you checked all your facts so that you are sure they are correct?

Can you add details that will make the story or report more entertaining or informative?

Are there any unclear passages in your writing? Should you substitute more precise language or swap in synonyms for overused words?

Look at the order of the information. Can you rearrange ideas to make them clearer? Can any unnecessary words be deleted?

Also, have a partner review your draft and give you feedback. Your partner might point out a part that is not clear and give suggestions for making changes.

Smooth Sentences

Be sure to include both long and short sentences to add interest to your writing.
If you find that you have several short, choppy sentences in a row, join them together into one longer sentence. Here is an example.

FIRST DRAFT	Students should not talk in the hall. Other classes can hear them. That's distracting.
REVISED	*Students should not talk in the hall because other classes can hear them and become distracted from their work.*

Take a look at Fiona's first draft of a story about her kitten. Can you help her revise her work?

FIRST DRAFT	I have a new kitten. Her name is Layla. She is 10 weeks old. Layla has fluffy black fur. One paw is white. We got her yesterday. She is little. She is scared. She hid under the couch.
REVISED	

Choose Your Words Wisely

Nouns are words that name people, places, animals, and things. Good writers choose strong, precise nouns to make their writing clear and interesting. Look at the nouns in each sentence below. See how precise nouns give the reader more information.

> FIRST DRAFT ▸▸ **He saw a dog.**
>
> REVISED ▸▸ **The paperboy saw a police dog.**

Verbs are words that tell the action in a sentence. When you write, choose vivid verbs that will help your reader picture exactly what is happening.

> FIRST DRAFT ▸▸ **Julie ate lunch.**
>
> REVISED ▸▸ **Julie devoured her lunch.**

Using **adjectives** to describe things can help make writing more clear and precise.

> FIRST DRAFT ▸▸ **Jack saw a bird.**
>
> REVISED ▸▸ **Jack saw an enormous bald eagle.**

Good writers use **adverbs** to tell more about something that happens in a story or other writing.

> FIRST DRAFT ▸▸ **Henry handed in his report.**
>
> REVISED ▸▸ **Henry proudly handed in his report.**

Add Details

Adding details will make your writing more interesting. Notice how details add meaning to the second sentence.

> **The skater glided.** ▸▸ **The graceful skater glided across the frozen lake.**

Punch It Up

> The sentences below are pretty basic. You could picture each scene more easily if the writer provided more information about the people, places, and things in the sentences. Add more information to each one.

Paul walked in. _____

Roses smell nice. _____

The movie was good. _____

Juliet bought new shoes. _____

The place was crowded. _____

Those bananas are brown. _____

PROOFREAD

Top Tips from Proofreaders

Find and Fix Errors

Now that you're done editing your writing for content, it is time to make sure that there are no misspellings and no incorrect grammar. To proofread your piece, reread your revised paper several times. Check for different types of errors each time.

Proofreading Steps

Check for punctuation errors. Be sure you used commas and end punctuation correctly.

Check each sentence for correct capitalization. Be sure you have capitals for street names, city names, and people's names.

Check for grammar and usage errors. Be sure your sentences are complete. Each one should have a subject, a verb, and some other information.

Check for spelling mistakes. Read your paper from the bottom to the top, word for word, to spot errors more easily. Circle any words you are unsure of. Check their spellings in the dictionary.

Here are a few suggestions for finding and fixing mistakes in your writing.

TAKE A BREAK Before you proofread, set your writing aside for a couple of hours. You will be more likely to catch mistakes if you take a break and return to your writing later with a clear mind.

PRINT IT OUT It is often easier to catch mistakes on paper than on screen. For proofreading, print out your work, mark the corrections on paper, and then enter the corrections on the computer.

TAKE YOUR TIME Consider each sentence as an individual thought. Does each sentence have a subject and a predicate? If not, add the missing sentence part.

READ OUT LOUD Read the piece of writing that you are editing aloud to yourself. This is a great way to "hear" whether your writing makes sense. Does the punctuation mark at the end of each sentence match the sound of your voice as you read?

SHARE YOUR WRITING Have a partner, friend, or family member read your work. Ask that person to comment on things he or she likes and doesn't like.

LOOK OUT!

Remember that computer spell-check programs catch some mistakes but not all of them. For example, if you write *their* instead of *they're*, the spell-checker will not point it out. A spell-checker will not point out words that have been left out of a sentence either.

Common Proofreading Marks

Proofreading is like detective work. Writers learn to look carefully to find and correct mistakes in their writing. Writers use a special set of marks to show what changes need to be made.

Symbol	What Does It Mean?	Example
≡	Make a capital letter.	Cousin <u>martha</u>≡ came to visit.
/	Make a lowercase letter.	She shared a room with my /Sister.
∧	Insert a letter or a word.	Martha and my sister ∧*are* the same age.
⊙	Add a period.	They look more like sisters than cousins⊙
⌃、	Add a comma.	Martha ⌃ my sister ⌃ and I like the same TV shows.
ℓ	Take this out.	We don't never want to go to sleep.
¶	Start a new paragraph.	Martha snored all night. ¶ The next morning, we made pancakes.
#	Add a space.	My sister#spilled syrup all over the table.

YOUR TURN!

Clean Up This Card!

Jasmine was in a hurry when she wrote this postcard to a friend. Correct her mistakes using proofreading marks.

Dear Katie

My grandparents don't have internet can you believe that? They don't have tv either but they do have alot of animals. I get up early to help them milk the cows. There are three of them and their names are betsy, gertrude and miss moo. Then I go to the chickencoop to see if there are any eggs and this is all before breakfast! I miss you

Love

Jasmine

157

PUBLISH

Be Selective

Good writers do not publish everything they write. They publish only their best writing.

Publishing Your Work

You spent a lot of time and effort on your writing. Now it's time to **publish,** or share, your work with others. This last part of the writing process can be a lot of fun. Depending on what you wrote, you might choose to post it on a class website, or e-mail it to friends and family. You could even make it into a booklet to save and share with your children and grandchildren someday! Here are some tips for getting your writing to look its best.

Create a Good Look

Pay close attention to how your writing looks on the page.

Fonts

Use different fonts, or print styles, to add interest to your writing. Here are just a few of the fonts that you may want to try.

This font is called Helvetica.

This font is called Courier.

This font is called Times New Roman.

This font is called Tahoma.

This font is called Georgia.

This font is called Futura.

Use one font for the main body of your writing. You may want to use a different font for the headline or title. Using three or more fonts in one piece of writing can look busy and messy. Avoid fonts that have lots of swirls or are hard to read. You want your writing to be clear, and you want the font you choose to be clear too.

Font Size

Choose a type size that makes your writing easy to read. Twelve-point type works well in most fonts and most kinds of writing. Use larger type, bold, and italics to make headlines and titles stand out. Compare these type sizes.

8-point type
10-point type
12-point type
14-point type
20-point type
36-point type

The main text font used in this book is Garamond.

Design

Begin with a title page. Center the title and type your name below it. If it is appropriate, consider adding graphic illustrations or designs to the pages.

Add Graphics

There is a saying "A picture is worth a thousand words." Adding picture elements to your writing can help you get your point across, but only if you choose your images wisely.

Photographs Adding photographs is a good choice if your writing is nonfiction. Visit online clip-art libraries or free stock-photography collections to find images of people, places, animals, or events in history. If you come across photos in the books you use as resources, you can scan and convert them into a digital format. But remember, images are copyrighted. That means they belong to someone. Only use images that are free and available to download. The Library of Congress (*loc.gov/pictures*) has a huge library of historical images that are available for use. If you are writing about something you did or saw yourself, you could include your own digital photos.

Illustrations Drawing your own illustrations makes sense if you write a story. You can also find clip art online. Another fun option is to partner with a friend or classmate who likes to draw. He or she could illustrate the story for you.

Tables and Charts To give readers more information about your topic, consider adding tables and charts. They present facts in a clear way that is easy to understand. For example, bar graphs can be useful for showing the results of surveys and the facts about "how many."

HOST A READING
Another way to share your work is to read it to others. If you have friends or classmates who like to write, get together and host a storytelling series. Perhaps you would consider reading some of your stories to kids at a local library. Talk to your parents, teachers, and friends about your writing, and ask for their advice on other places where you might perform or read your work.

PAGE 8: SHOW WHAT YOU KNOW

- Nick helped Mr. Preston make a (sign) for the (carnival) in Springdale.
- Linda knows that (education) is important in South Africa.
- There is no (school) on Monday because it is Presidents' Day.
- Grandpa Jack was too young to fight in the Vietnam War.
- Kim and Anna are identical (twins).
- Jack did his (report) on (penguins) in Antarctica.

PAGE 9: A PROPER MATCHUP

Common Nouns	Proper Nouns
boy	Taj Mahal
road	November
dog	Mount Everest
president	Fourth of July
holiday	Fred
continent	Oakdale Lane
month	Chihuahua
monument	North America
mountain	Barack Obama

PAGE 9: KNOW YOUR NOUNS

1. Camp Wamsutta
2. Eric
3. July
4. Felicity
5. Grandpa Jim
6. Saturday

PAGE 10: FROM NOUN TO NOUNS

valley ▸ valleys
reef ▸ reefs
nose ▸ noses
toe ▸ toes
toy ▸ toys

lunch ▸ lunches
watch ▸ watches
beach ▸ beaches
fox ▸ foxes
buzz ▸ buzzes

library ▸ libraries
country ▸ countries
family ▸ families
berry ▸ berries
penny ▸ pennies

PAGE 11: IRREGULAR PLURALS

one child
  ▸▸ several children
one mouse
  ▸▸ three blind mice
one tooth
  ▸▸ all my teeth
calf ▸ calves
hoof ▸ hooves
wolf ▸ wolves

PAGE 11: HOW MANY?

Special Plural	Singular
tomatoes	tomato
oxen	ox
thieves	thief
geese	goose
feet	foot
loaves	loaf

PAGE 12: MAKE IT POSSESSIVE

- Mary is wearing a hat. Mary's hat has a feather in it.
- It took a long time for the jury to reach a decision. The jury's verdict was guilty.
- Kendall has twin sisters. His sisters' birthday is May 15.
- The architect drew up plans for a new house. There were three balconies in the architect's plans.
- The animal shelter had four cages for rabbits. The rabbits' cages were in the back room.
- Three women went out for lunch together. A waiter brought the women's menus.
- The dog jumped over the fence. The dog's collar came off.

PAGE 17: PICK YOUR PRONOUNS

- Louisa and I are going shopping.
- Kyle and they are at the arcade.
- We and they went out to dinner together.
- Dad told me to clean my room.
- She and Jackson were science partners.
- Mom already picked them up.
- My grandparents took us to a movie.

PAGE 19: REFLECT ON THIS

- Susan bought *herself* a birthday present.
- I taught *myself* how to play the piano.
- No one will win if they all vote for *themselves*.
- We helped *ourselves* to dessert.
- After his haircut, Jake did not recognize *himself* in the mirror.

PAGE 26: IN THE PAST? OR IN THE FUTURE?

Past Tense	Future Tense
called	will call
appeared	will appear
stayed	will stay
climbed	will climb
cooked	will cook

PAGE 29: SHOW AND TELL

Last week, Ms. Goldman *spoke* to the class about being kind to animals. The last time she spoke to us, she *brought* a dog with her. This time she *held* up an iguana in a cage to show the class! Some people were frightened, but Ms. Goldman *said* there was nothing to worry about. She *told* us that iguanas get along well with people. She even *kept* an iguana as a pet when she was a little girl.

PAGE 21: SPOTTING ACTION VERBS

Charlotte and Darren danced in their school's talent show. First, Charlotte twirled around the room. Then Darren leaped across the stage. He hopped and jumped all around. Charlotte and Darren swayed to the music and sang along with the lyrics. When the music stopped, they stopped. The other students stood while they clapped and cheered. Charlotte and Darren smiled at each other. They reached for each other's hand, and then they bowed and left the stage.

PAGE 28: TO BE OR NOT TO BE . . .

Gina and her family <u>are</u> in Boston on their vacation. They <u>are</u> interested in the history of the old city. It <u>is</u> more than 350 years old. In those early days, some streets of Boston <u>were</u> only dirt paths. There <u>were</u> no traffic lights on any corners! "That <u>was</u> my favorite trip ever," Gina said when they got home.

I *was* surprised to see that Boston *is* a modern city. There *are* tall buildings made of steel and glass right next to smaller, older brick buildings. Yesterday, we *were* so tired of walking that we took the subway to see Paul Revere's house. Boston's subway *is* the oldest subway system in the United States! Our guide at Paul Revere's house *was* from Ohio, just like us! There *are* people here from all over the world!

PAGE 30: FAMILY PHOTOS

Great-Aunt Sylvie <u>has lived</u> in the same house all her life. On Saturday, Margaret and her mother <u>will visit</u> there. They <u>are taking</u> recent family photos with them, and Great-Aunt Sylvie <u>will show</u> them an old family album. Margaret <u>is looking</u> forward to the visit.

PAGE 31: QUICK LEARNER

Jennifer has <u>enjoyed</u> listening to music for a long time. She has <u>studied</u> piano for one year. I have <u>heard</u> better players, but they have all <u>studied</u> for many years. Jennifer has <u>become</u> a very good player in only a year. She has always <u>wanted</u> to play as well as famous piano players. She has <u>promised</u> to learn my favorite song. Jennifer and her friends have <u>talked</u> about playing for an audience. They have <u>mentioned</u> this plan to many people!

161

PAGE 31: FORMING A BAND

For months now, Dave and Michael _have_ wanted to start a band. Dave _has_ played the drums for several years. Michael received a guitar on his birthday and _has_ plucked its strings every day since then. The boys _have_ started regular practice sessions together. They are still looking for a singer, and I _have_ thought about trying out for the position! I _have_ wanted to sing in a band for a long time!

PAGE 33: STORYTELLING WORDS

Wayne has 11 adjectives, and Cristina has 10, so Wayne has more.

PAGE 34: DESCRIBE AND COMPARE

My backpack is heavy, but her backpack is _heavier_.
All kittens are small, but the runt of the litter is the _smallest_.
My room is clean, but my sister's room is _cleaner_.
The neighbors have three smelly dogs, and the one named King is the _smelliest_.

PAGE 35: MAKE THE MOST OF IT

Adjective (Positive Form)	Comparative Form	Superlative Form
dirty	dirtier	dirtiest
interesting	more interesting	most interesting
safe	safer	safest
peaceful	more peaceful	most peaceful
awesome	more awesome	most awesome
proud	prouder	proudest
enormous	more enormous	most enormous
smooth	smoother	smoothest

PAGE 37: COMPARATIVE CROSSWORD CHALLENGE

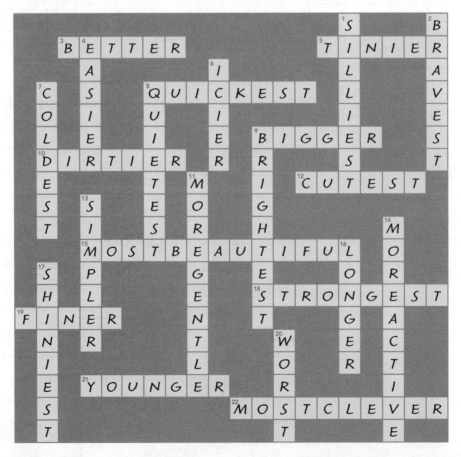

PAGE 38: COMMA COMMANDER

- Sheila bought a cute red miniskirt at the mall yesterday. ✓
- Ms. Pearson has a busy demanding job as a veterinarian.
- That restaurant serves the lightest fluffiest pancakes I ever tasted.
- We just drove past an old stone house. ✓
- After sledding, Tyson took a long hot shower. ✓
- Jane and I just had a stupid pointless argument over nothing.

PAGE 39: WHICH COMES FIRST?

Last summer, we went on a long, exhausting camping trip.
I want a huge three-layer chocolate birthday cake.
She wore size-8 black Italian leather shoes.

PAGE 43: TRY IT IN A SENTENCE

Here are the correct spellings of the adverbs. Sentences will vary.

gracefully
mysteriously
nervously
lazily
awkwardly
eagerly

PAGE 44: DESCRIPTIVE DUOS

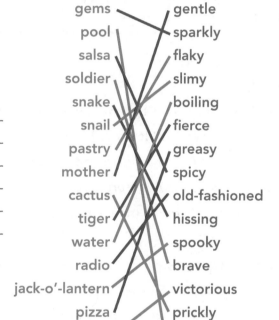

gems — gentle
pool — sparkly
salsa — flaky
soldier — slimy
snake — boiling
snail — fierce
pastry — greasy
mother — spicy
cactus — old-fashioned
tiger — hissing
water — spooky
radio — brave
jack-o'-lantern — victorious
pizza — prickly
team — shallow

PAGE 45: ADVERB JUMBLE

daylitemime = *immediately*
yuledeepnxct = *unexpectedly*
rullygear = *regularly*
nailfly = *finally*
yooshfill = *foolishly*
futtyorlean = *fortunately*
tallcandyice = *accidentally*
saylaw = *always*
soyajulle = *jealously*
hulyring = *hungrily*
lganiry = *angrily*

PAGE 46: BRINGING SENTENCES TOGETHER

- I like fruit, *and* I like cookies.
- Jeb studied for the math test, *so* he aced it.
- Katie packed her bag, *so* she was ready to go.
- Nathan speaks Spanish and English, *but* Luis speaks only Spanish.
- The school bus was late, *so* Alice was late for school.
- Lisa slept over at Grandma's house, *but* her brother stayed home.
- Peggy Sue likes scary movies, *but* Billy does not like them.

PAGE 48: PICK OUT THE PREPOSITIONS

Our school has a chess club. It meets <u>on</u> Tuesdays <u>after</u> school <u>for</u> an hour. The members study the rules <u>of</u> the game and talk <u>about</u> different strategies <u>for</u> playing well. <u>Before</u> a tournament, the club members meet <u>for</u> practice games. <u>During</u> the games, the players concentrate hard. I am thinking <u>about</u> joining the chess club.

PAGE 49: FIELD TRIP FILL-IN

Here is one way to complete this paragraph.

This morning, all the Nature Club members climbed _inside_ a bus bound _for_ our town's nature preserve. Once there, everyone hiked the marked trails _through_ the woods. Mr. Cindiric was _ahead of_ the group. He is an expert _about_ all the different birds, animals, and plants _in_ this area. He taught us to look _above_ our heads for birds' nests. We saw a mother bird feeding her babies, but _beneath_ the tree, we saw some tiny broken eggs. As the group walked _along_ the shore of the lake, Mr. Cindiric showed us a raccoon's paw prints.

PAGE 49: FROM START TO FINISH

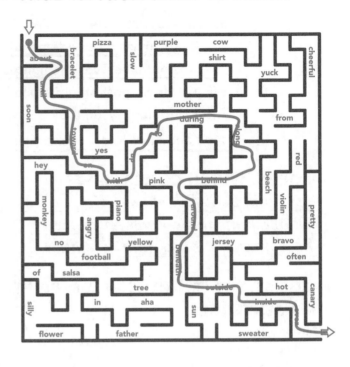

PAGE 54: SENTENCE SPOTTER

Can you name an animal that is bigger than an elephant? I will give you a hint. It can swim. Now do you know what it is? It is the blue whale. Did you know a blue whale can grow to be 100 feet long? It can weigh as much as a dozen elephants. That's a lot! When it is born, a baby blue whale can be as large as an elephant. Don't try to play with one!

PAGE 55: MIX AND MATCH ZEBRA TALES

Herds of zebras — confuse predators.

A zebra's blended stripes — can reach 40 miles per hour.

The running speed of a zebra — was hunted to extinction by humans.

A zebra's powerful kick — are dangerous predators of zebras.

Human hunters — is forceful enough to kill a lion.

One species of zebra — were mostly brown and had few stripes.

These extinct zebras — have ways of defending themselves against predators.

PAGE 56: PLAY I SPY WITH SIMPLE SUBJECTS AND PREDICATES

Harry Houdini became a great escape artist. He picked many different kinds of locks. People tied him in ropes and handcuffs. Houdini always escaped. His most dangerous trick happened underwater. People locked him in chains. They then threw him into a river. Houdini escaped from the chains. Then he swam to the surface of the water. Many people watched this trick.

PAGE 56: COMPLETE SUBJECTS VS. COMPOUND SUBJECTS

<u>Warm-blooded animals</u> are able to keep their body temperature constant. (Birds and mammals) are warm-blooded. <u>These animals</u> can turn the food they eat into energy. <u>This complicated process</u> creates heat. <u>Some warm-blooded animals</u> sweat when they get too hot. (Dogs and wolves) pant to cool down.

PAGE 57: COMPLETE PREDICATES VS. COMPOUND PREDICATES

Cold-blooded animals <u>have the same temperature as their surroundings</u>. They (move and hunt) in hot weather. Chemicals in their bodies <u>react quickly to help</u> <u>their muscles move</u>. These reactions slow down as the outside temperature drops. So they (move slowly or stay still) at low temperatures.

PAGE 57: LABELING LESSON

CS Plants and animals are the two largest kingdoms of life.

___ The animal kingdom includes both tiny and huge animals.

CP Some animals see and hear better than humans.

CP Biologists study and classify animals.

CP Animals eat and digest food.

___ Vertebrates have a bony skeleton and a backbone.

CS Amphibians and reptiles are vertebrates.

CP Some frogs shed and eat their skin.

B Alligators and crocodiles look and act alike.

CS Birds and fish are also vertebrates.

B Bald eagles and other birds of prey hunt and eat small animals.

CS Carp and eels are examples of fish.

CP Most fish live and lay eggs in water.

CS Mushrooms, mold, and mildew are fungi.

PAGE 59: CAN IT STAND ALONE?

I stayed home from school (because) I had a cold. (After) I took my medicine, I felt better. I napped (while) Mom did chores. (Even though) I was still a little sick, Mom took me with her to the supermarket. I pushed the shopping cart (while) Mom chose the vegetables. Mom bought three bags of oranges (because) they were on sale. She would have bought oranges (even if) they were not on sale. Oranges are good to eat (when) you have a cold.

PAGE 59: PINPOINTING PREPOSITIONAL PHRASES

<u>In the spring</u>, a famous race is run <u>in the city</u> <u>of Boston</u>. The name <u>of the</u> <u>race</u> is the Boston Marathon. Runners come <u>from many countries</u>. The hardest part is running <u>up the hills</u>. The athletes run <u>through several towns</u> <u>on their way</u> <u>to the city</u>. <u>Along the route</u>, the athletes run <u>with different people</u>. Supporters <u>on the street</u> cheer <u>for the</u> <u>dedicated competitors</u>.

PAGE 61: **BEST BUDDIES**

Ethan and Luke grew up together they went to the same school. The boys liked the same sports they played soccer in the fall and basketball in the winter. Some people thought the boys were brothers they looked so much alike. Ethan's mother and Luke's mother were best friends. The two families even went on vacations together sometimes they went camping.

There is more than one way to correct each run-on sentence.

PAGE 63: **MAKE IT WORK!**

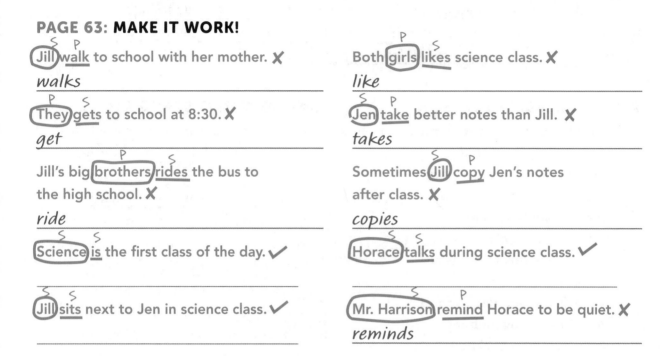

Jill walk to school with her mother. ✗
walks

They gets to school at 8:30. ✗
get

Jill's big brothers rides the bus to the high school. ✗
ride

Science is the first class of the day. ✓

Jill sits next to Jen in science class. ✓

Both girls likes science class. ✗
like

Jen take better notes than Jill. ✗
takes

Sometimes Jill copy Jen's notes after class. ✗
copies

Horace talks during science class. ✓

Mr. Harrison remind Horace to be quiet. ✗
reminds

PAGE 64: **ARE WE ALL IN AGREEMENT?**

- Paul and his brothers *go* to the same school.
- Either Paul's brothers or his sister *brings* in the newspaper.
- Either Paul's sister or his brothers *bring* in the newspaper.
- The boys and their dog *walk* around the block every evening.
- Lauren or her sisters *win* every race they enter.
- Cats or a dog *is* allowed in that apartment building.

PAGE 67: **WHICH PRONOUNS WORK?**

Mr. Smith *he, him, his, himself*
a book *it, its*
grandparents *they, their, them, themselves*

Mrs. McGee *she, her, hers, herself*
flowers *they, them*
a mouse *it, its, itself*
brothers *they, their, them, themselves*

PAGE 68: SHOULDN'T HE STUDY HIS LINES?

Gary and Lenny are trying out for the same part in the class play. One boy (isn't) going to get the part. (Nobody) knows whom the director will choose. Gary has (never) been in a play before. He does (not) want to make a mistake while he is trying out. Lenny hopes that he (won't) be disappointed, but he (hasn't) studied his lines. The director will (not) be happy about that!

PAGE 69: DON'T FALL INTO THE DOUBLE NEGATIVE TRAP!

The play that our class is putting on is about a jewel thief and a detective. The jewel thief is (anyone/no one) you would want to know. He is dishonest and mean. The detective doesn't seem to have (any/no) luck in her pursuit of the thief. The thief never leaves clues when he robs a mansion. He hasn't even left behind (no/one) fingerprint. At first, the detective doesn't have (no/any) luck, but then the jewel thief makes a mistake. He wants to break into a safe, but he can't find (no/any) gloves (anywhere/nowhere)!

PAGE 69: WARNING: DOUBLE NEGATIVES AHEAD

A double negative can be fixed in more than one way. Here are some options.

She can't have no more pie.
She can't have any more pie.

I didn't break no one's window.
I didn't break anyone's window.

Don't never do that again!
Don't do that again! / Never do that again!

I don't get no respect.
I don't get any respect. / I get no respect.

I can't write no more.
I can't write anymore.

PAGE 72: NUMBER KNOW-HOW

- Dogs have *four* legs, but people have only *two*.
- Thomas was absent *eight* days over a period of *three* months.
- Kylie watched *60* airplanes take off while she waited *30* minutes for her flight to board.
- Harry visited *17* websites to find the information he needed to answer the *20* social studies questions.
- My family has *one* dog, *three* cats, *two* birds, and *twenty-three (or 23)* tropical fish.

PAGE 75: TITLE TUNE-UP

One Direction's first single, "What Makes You Beautiful," was released in the U.K. in September 2011 and shot to the top of the charts. The group released its first U.S. album, Up All Night, on March 13, 2012. Billboard magazine reported that the album was an immediate hit. Later, the group was on the TV show iCarly. The singers made a special appearance on the episode called "iGo One Direction." After releasing the album Take Me Home, in November 2012, they set out on a massive world tour, traveling through Europe, Australia, and North America.

PAGE 79: SHORTENED SEARCH-A-WORD

```
Y A W K R A P A S R X E I J A T I X A P R M C V E
C L D N K G B L G Q Z K L Q R Z T O E M F I G C P
E D W I E P E P V Y I P M L P W L J I H R O X M D
C V Z W E A R K A N S A S Z O G M K S G I F R P T
X I L F L R M L O O C E E U A C I U P C D E C T I
O H F N E D C O C H Z R N O I V S N D I A T D I D
U B C C H S O E A U X F A I E P S Y E L Y Z A V L
J T M P Z S Y C P N I F T M A O O I A Q U G I R O
I N F I O I X L T Y N R O A D G U K S D Z L O E A
A O J T F H Q I A O M V R E I Q R E R N S E D I E
K V E E K Q E E I N R H B U O E I P H Z B E K V G
A E C U I R X M N H U A I F A P T E V H E Z U T Z
V M I S T E R B O A W R A O G T Z S U M A T S T I
E B O Y Q I J I B K S S O E U R U N E O F H K W H
I E E P S T F G H T C G D F P J H R X U Q C X L E
J R V P X K I F E B I V U R C A N K D N I K A I O
K L C K R E V Z O N Q J E O Z N D U S T R E E T H
N E I C E O I L L I N O I S M U P Q M O T O I S N
O N A F F N S R U Y E S P Y U A Y O P E C L U A E
U L R O I O T P K H A M E S E R G E A N T H E B F
S D X L C K M U B M Z H J E U Y P R O F E S S O R
I E U O V E Z L C O E I Y L B V A L S P I U L P O
R G H H O Q O Y R K M U E J O I Z O X Z M O S X V
Z X C V F P L Z B M Y O S N E S B A E X C A A E P
S E Q B O U L E V A R D O X J U L P F J N U O N F
```

PAGE 83: PICK YOUR PUNCTUATION

- How old were you when you lost your first baby tooth *?*
- Jack learned how to make a worm box in science class *.*
- No one really knows what happens during time travel *.*
- What is the capital of Iowa *?*
- I know why you said that *!*
- Emma wishes she knew why her socks keep disappearing *.*
- Don't touch that wire *!*
- When is our social studies project due *?*
- Jane accidentally left her sweatshirt at the library *.*
- Look, there's a shooting star *!*

PAGE 84: FOLLOW THE ARROWS

PAGE 85: A WONDROUS PLANT

What is — the smallest flower in the world?

Its common name is — watermeal.

The plant itself is about — the size of one candy sprinkle.

That's — amazing plant!

How much does — it weigh?

It weighs — as much as only two grains of table salt!

Where does — it live?

This unusual plant floats — on the surface of calm, fresh water.

What an — tiny!

PAGE 86: USE YOUR EAGLE EYES

- My full name is Clarkson Kensington Royce, but my friends call me C.K.
- My alarm clock must be broken because it went off at 4 a.m.
- Mr. and Mrs. Hendricks just got a new dog.
- J.K. Rowling is my favorite author.
- Sally counted 243 pennies for a total of $2.43.

PAGE 87: TESTING, TESTING

- You (do)/don't put a period after initials in a person's name.
- You do/(don't) have two periods at the end of a sentence.
- You (do)/don't end a statement about a question with a period.
- You do/(don't) end a question with a period.

PAGE 87: WHAT'S MISSING?

I went to my local bookstore on Saturday around 1 p.m. to find a book for my book report. I picked out *Wonder*, by R.J. Palacio. The librarian, Ms. Thomas, was very helpful. She recommended a series of books called The Sisters Grimm, by Michael Buckley. I bought three books, which cost $31.27 all together. The bookstore is on Washington St. There are so many fantastic books there! You should check it out.

PAGE 91: COMMA QUEST

- Mariska won first place at the science fair.
- Yuck, I wish the cat would use its litter box.
- You're right, the capital of South Dakota is Pierre.
- My goodness, you've grown a foot and a half since I last saw you.
- Jack likes going out to eat, but he only likes Chinese restaurants.
- If you say that again, I'm going to scream.
- Pat went out for ice cream after the movie.
- I told Jeff to take out the trash.
- Peggy Sue wanted a good grade, so she studied hard for the math test.
- Although Olga tried her best, she did not win the geography bee.
- While walking to school, Ingrid accidentally stepped on a caterpillar.

PAGE 92: WHERE DID ALL THE COMMAS GO?

- Fred bought notebooks, pencils, pens, markers, and book covers at the back-to-school sale.
- A good diet includes fruits, vegetables, and grains, as well as high-protein foods, such as eggs, meat, dairy, fish, and chicken.
- Justin put forks, knives, and spoons on the table.
- Ceci found socks, shoes, and an old sandwich under her bed.
- Katie got a necklace, a bag of candy, and two books for her birthday.

PAGE 95: THE GREAT COMMA CHALLENGE

- Francie wanted a part in the play, so she auditioned.
- When Francie entered the auditorium, the auditions had already begun.
- My dog sleeps on a pillow, barks in its sleep, and wakes up hungry.
- When I was nine and my sister was a baby, I helped her get dressed.
- The sun set in the western sky, and the full moon rose in the east.
- Jack was a self-respecting, intelligent teenager.
- Rebecca doesn't like speaking in front of a group, even her classmates.
- As the soccer ball was flying toward the goal, Jimmy tried to block it.
- It would help, you know, if you said you were sorry.
- If everyone recycled more, we might not need a new landfill.

PAGE 96: X MARKS THE SPOT

- Paul collects stamps and coins: from many other countries. ✗
- Max and his class were studying human biology in science class, including: the digestive system, the nervous system, and the brain. ✗
- These boys made the basketball team: Luke, Ethan, Kevin, Kyle, Andrew, Gus, Michael, and Logan. ✓
- Camp Pocahontas encourages campers to participate in all the activities offered: horseback riding, swimming, canoeing, crafts, ball sports, and archery. ✓
- Some personality traits are helpful: when dealing with difficult people, patience, empathy, compassion, and a good sense of humor. ✗

- Claire made the following for the school bake sale: an apple tart, brownies, a sheet cake with lemon frosting, and a dozen cupcakes.
- Gina forgot to set her alarm clock, overslept, and was late for work.
- Marnie likes only three flavors of ice cream: vanilla, strawberry, and chocolate.
- There are many places to go skiing near Brattleboro, Vermont.
- Amanda has four sisters: Brianna, Mychaela, Rhonda, and Ashley.
- Al and Tony argued yesterday, but today, they are back to being best friends.
- Three teachers were out today with the flu: Mr. Meek, Mrs. Ferland, and Mr. Harrison.
- Today's lunch options are pizza, chicken nuggets, fruit, and salad.
- Anton remembered all the state capitals except for three: Rhode Island, New Jersey, and New Mexico.

PAGE 98: **MATCH AND JOIN**

Grapes were on sale at the supermarket; Mom bought two bags.

Fred was having a party Friday night; he bought chips and salsa.

Lisa felt sick during second period; she went to the nurse's office.

Patrick lives far away; it takes him an hour to get to school.

Daylight saving time started yesterday; we set our clocks ahead one hour.

It snowed heavily last night; school was canceled.

PAGE 99: **COOL CONNECTORS**

There is more than one correct answer. Here is one option for each sentence pair.

Paulette woke up in the middle of the night; eventually, she fell back asleep.

Russell forgot the combination; as a result, he could not open his locker.

Johnnie forgot to water the plant; consequently, it died.

The man had an alibi; nevertheless, the jury still found him guilty.

Kim liked peanut butter; as a result, she ate the entire jar in one sitting.

Kylie wanted a puppy; however, her parents decided to adopt a kitten.

The trash was beginning to stink; finally, Trevor put it in the Dumpster.

PAGE 102: **INSERT A THOUGHT**

There is more than one correct answer. Here is one option for each sentence pair.

Lois Lane (Superman's girlfriend) is a comic-book character.

I have an aunt (her name is Agatha) who lives in Poughkeepsie.

There is a poem (written by someone famous) about Paul Revere.

One of the mugs (the one with the pink turtle) is chipped.

PAGE 102: A PUNCTUATION MYSTERY

- Koo and her husband own a farm; they grow vegetables.
- Kathleen put tomatoes (they were organic) on her sandwich.
- Alstead, New Hampshire, is a small town, but it does have its own middle school.
- Only one student (I think it was Felicity) got a perfect score on the math test.

- The public library has a young adult section; that's where you can find books by Rick Riordan and Scott Westerfeld.
- John forgot his gym clothes, so his mother dropped off his shorts, socks, and sneakers during lunch.
- Lou's parents are both doctors; they work at the same hospital in downtown Cleveland.

PAGE 103: THE GREAT PUNCTUATION RACE

- There was a fly in the soup.
- The waiter was embarrassed; he apologized.
- The waiter brought another bowl of soup to the table, and he apologized again.
- The chef (wearing a tall white hat) came out of the kitchen to make sure everyone was happy.

PAGE 107: WHOSE IS THIS?

- Mom found my brother's baseball mitt under the bed.
- I can't do my homework without my textbook.
- Olga found her mother's car keys in the refrigerator.
- He's very sorry he broke your window.
- Ned stayed overnight at Brian's house.
- Most toddlers don't know how to tie their shoes.
- Grandma's recipe uses buttermilk instead of sour cream.

PAGE 105: QUOTATION FIXER-UPPERS

- "Benjamin Franklin," our teacher explained, "was one of the Founding Fathers of our country."
- "That's me in the picture," she said.
- My grandparents have an old recording of Frank Sinatra singing "My Way."
- Aunt Harriet asked me to "pick up her mail" while she's out of town.
- "Did you take out the trash?" Dad asked.
- The captain said, "I hope you don't get seasick," and handed me a bucket just in case.

PAGE 112: HYPHEN CHECK

- Mom, when we go to the park, can I ride the merry-go-round? X
- My step-brother practices karate. X
- I used wood and paint to recreate the sign that was knocked down. X
- For the school dance, I have chosen a purplish-blue tie. X
- Kim is a well-read nine-year-old girl. ✓
- The homework assignment on Marie Curie (1867-1934) is on pages 62-68. ✓

PAGE 113: CURIOUS ABOUT HYPHENS?

There is no dream too big for NASA's Jet Propuls-
ion Laboratory (JPL). Since it was formed in 1936,
JPL has pushed the limits of exploration. By focu-
sing primarily on the making of robotic space-
craft, this team has repeatedly made histor-
y. Currently, the Mars Science Laboratory
is one of JPL's largest missions. For decades,
the team has been sending instruments, de-
vices, and robots to the Red Planet to deter-
mine if there has ever been life on Mars. In November 2011, JPL sent a high-tech rover called
Curiosity to Mars. The journey was 285 million mil-
es (459 million km) long and took eight months.

PAGE 115: MAKE YOUR MARK!

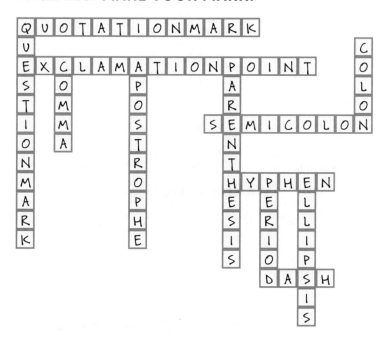

PAGE 121: SHOW OFF YOUR SKILLS!

- I don't know *who's* at the door.
- The dog slipped out of *its* collar.
- Phil, is it okay if I give Gail *your* e-mail address?
- I know *it's* Saturday, but I still have to go to work.
- I know *they're* your grandparents, but they seem too young.
- I can wait till *you're* done eating breakfast.
- The twins left *their* bathing suits at the pool.
- Do you know *whose* phone this is?
- *There's* a spot on my new dress.
- I took mine, not *yours*.
- Please sit over *there*.

PAGE 119: WHICH ONE WON?

- They spent the *whole* day filling in that *hole* in the ground.
- The soccer team *won* only *one* game this year.
- Carlos had the flu and felt *weak* all *week*.
- Rita hated to *waste* food, but she wanted a smaller *waist*.
- The butchers agreed to *meet* at the *meat* market.
- Wendy went to the beach to *see* the *sea*.
- The person who delivers our *mail* is *male*.
- The greedy boy *ate eight* slices of cake.
- There is a *tale* about a fox who loses his *tail*.
- Sarah caught the *flu* after she *flew* in an airplane.
- Ouch, *I* got something in my *eye*.
- We were *bored*, so we played a *board* game.
- Gina did not mean to *break* the *brake* on her bicycle.
- It's so noisy, I can't *hear* you in *here*.
- Zack *blew* up a *blue* balloon for the birthday party.
- A *dear* friend went *deer* hunting.
- *Which witch* cast the spell?
- The *maid made* the bed.

PAGE 122: RIDDLE ME THIS

a bat
a nail
bark
a ruler

PAGE 123: PICTURE PAIRS

leaves

crane

duck

sheet

wave

PAGE 125: QUIRKY CROSSWORD

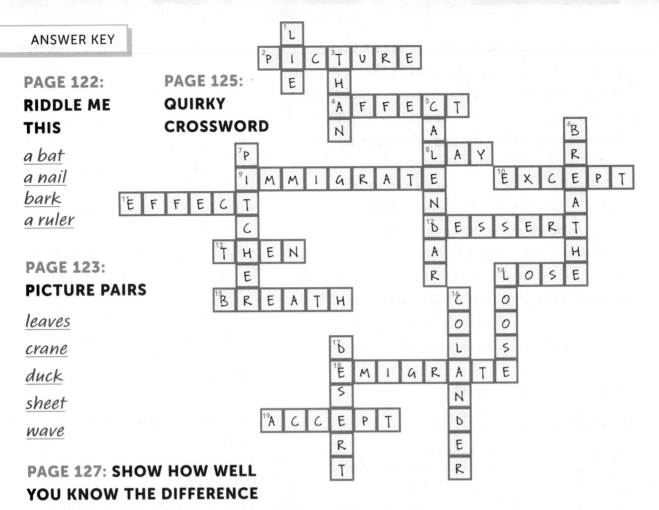

PAGE 127: SHOW HOW WELL YOU KNOW THE DIFFERENCE

- Jess doesn't speak Spanish very _well_.
- Walt had a _good_ time at the beach.
- It's _good_ to be here with you all for Thanksgiving.
- I wanted that cookie so _badly_.
- His new business did _well_ its first year.
- Too much sugar is _bad_ for you.

PAGE 129: WHAT'S THE RIGHT WORD?

- I did not know you were in town, or I would _have_ invited you to my party.
- Rebecca has eaten _fewer_ calories since she began her new diet.
- Jack felt _less_ self-conscious after he got his braces off.
- The weather did not _affect_ my decision to stay home on Saturday.
- When my dog curls up near my feet, I can feel its _breath_ on my ankles.
- Paula _scratched_ her chin whenever she was concentrating on a problem.
- The mosquito bite on her leg _itched_.

PAGE 131: TEST YOUR KNOWLEDGE

- Who cares, any way? X
- The twins are all ready to go. ✓
- Every one is invited to my party. X
- I maybe able to come to your party. X
- Nancy all ways wears her hair in a ponytail. X
- I can't find any body who took notes during that class. X
- My mother usually answers maybe when I ask her a question. ✓
- I will solve this problem any way I can! ✓
- Aidan all ready has a date for the prom. X

PAGE 132: BUILDING BLOCKS

Here are some of the new words you can make using the root words and suffixes listed.

actor	lifeless	selfish
editor	childlike	selfless
painter	childish	hopeful
dancer	childless	hopeless
blockage	governor	joyful
pilgrimage	government	joyless
lifer	friendship	careless
lifelike	friendless	careful

PAGE 135: DOUBLE UP!

- short _tall_
- prince _princess_
- on _off_
- empty _full_
- none _all_
- more _less_
- push _pull_
- buy _sell_
- sharp, exciting _dull_

PAGE 137: GIANT WORD SEARCH

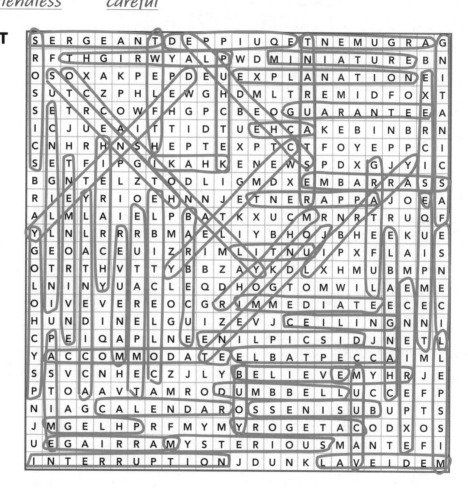

PAGE 157: CLEAN UP THIS CARD!

Dear katie,

My grandparents don't have internet, can you believe that?
They don't have a tv either, but they do have a lot of animals.
I get up early to help them milk the cows. There are three of
them and their names are betsy, gertrude and miss moo. Then I
go to the chicken coop to see if there are any eggs, and this is
all before breakfast! I miss you.

Love,
Jasmine

175